PRAISE FOR
THE CHARACTER OF GOD CONTROVERSY

"In the course of the great controversy Satan has pitted God's justice against His love. In heaven he told the angels that God was too just to forgive. Now many are teaching that God is too loving to destroy. *The Character of God Controversy* reveals—in the light of the Cross—that God's justice did not spare His own Son, but His love gave Him up for us all (Romans 8:32). A must read for those who are seeking a better understanding of God's character in these last days."

—Stephen Bohr, director of *Secrets Unsealed*

"The pendulum of popular opinion on the character of God has swung away from the 'fire and brimstone' extreme to the present vision of a benign Being who is too kind to risk causing us pain by punishing sin. This book corrects the current fallacies without going back to the other extreme."

—Robert Ford, MD, cofounder of *Pacific Cataract and Laser Institute*

"Wohlberg and Lewis have clearly, biblically, honestly, yet kindly, dealt head-on with the apparent dichotomy between God's justice and His mercy. Their total immersion into the agonizing sacrifice of Jesus Christ for our sins makes the book full of love, grace, and power. After reading it, you will agree with those standing on the sea of glass: ' "Just and true are Your ways, O King of the saints!" ' " (Revelation 15:3).

—Bill Krick, director of *California Youth Rush*

"This huge question about the character of God is very real, because most of us Christians, regardless of denomination, have a doctored image of Jesus. We practice 'Jesus-ol-atry,' creating our personal image of God/Jesus and bowing down to it. Most wince when we hear that God might be a Supreme Deity of justice and divine retribution. Unacceptable, we declare! Often, rather than quietly coming to grips with that aspect of divinity and what it might mean for us today on a personal basis, we make excuses. I suspect that a careful examination of this book will leave most (if not all) of us feeling at least a tad uncomfortable. And yet—thank the Lord!—this book also offers a heavenly solution for our guilt and sin."

—Lonnie Melashenko, speaker/director of the *Voice of Prophecy*

"In their exploration of God's love, mercy, and justice, Steve Wohlberg and Chris Lewis provide solid biblical evidence that God's wrath is more than a passive abandonment of sinners to their fate—though that is included. God's active wrath in dealing with sin and sinners is not a contradiction of divine love. The biblical evidence reveals that God's wrath is a *manifestation* of His love. This book makes a significant contribution to the current debate over God's character."

—Marvin Moore, editor, *Signs of the Times®*

"*The Character of God Controversy* is a timely and much needed work that reveals the true nature and balance of God's justice and mercy. Many sincere people have fallen into one of two ditches on either side of the track of truth, either presenting God as cruel vindictive ruler or as a God so loving that He never administers justice. This book will put and keep its readers squarely on the track of truth."

—Ivor Myers, *Power of the Lamb Ministries*

"*The Character of God Controversy* is a book that is long overdue. In a time when people run to extremes, it expounds a balanced portrayal of God's character. Many do not understand that all truth, as found in His word, is held in a divine-tension of seeming contradictions. This is seen in such attributes as justice and mercy; law and grace; love and hate. Trying to reconcile these seemly contradictory terms has caused confusion for some who seek to know God. This book is written in such a way that it will inspire those who seek deeper exegetical study, yet at the same time is 'user friendly' for the layman."

—Jeff Reich, speaker/director of *Laymen Ministries*

THE
CHARACTER
OF GOD
CONTROVERSY

THE CHARACTER OF GOD CONTROVERSY

*A Close Look at the Intense Love
and Justice of Almighty God*

STEVE WOHLBERG
& CHRIS LEWIS
FOREWORD BY G. EDWARD REID

Pacific Press® Publishing Association
Nampa, Idaho
Oshawa, Ontario, Canada
www.pacificpress.com

Cover design by Charles Lawson
Cover design resources from Darrin Brooks, sermonview.com
Inside design by Aaron Troia

Except where otherwise noted, all Scripture quotations are from the New King
James Version, copyright © 1979, 1980, 1982, Thomas Nelson, Inc., Publishers.

You can obtain additional copies of this book by calling toll-free 1-800-765-6955
or by visiting http://www.adventistbookcenter.com.

Library of Congress Cataloging-in-Publication Data
Wohlberg, Steve, 1959-
The character of God controversy : a close look at the intense love
and justice of Almighty God / Steve Wohlberg and Chris Lewis.
p. cm.
Includes bibliographical references.
ISBN-13: 978-0-8163-2288-6 (pbk.)
ISBN-10: 0-8163-2288-0 (pbk.)
1. Seventh-day Adventists—Doctrines. 2. Adventists—Doctrines. 3.
God. 4. White, Ellen Gould Harmon, 1827-1915. I. Lewis, Chris, 1975-
II. Title.
BX6154.W64 2008
231'.4—dc22
2008026098

08 09 10 11 12 • 5 4 3 2 1

ALSO BY STEVE WOHLBERG

Demons in Disguise: The Dangers of Talking to the Dead

Exposing Harry Potter and Witchcraft:
The Menace Behind the Magic

End Time Delusions:
The Rapture, the Antichrist, Israel, and the End of the World

From Hollywood to Heaven

The Hot Topic of Hell:
Separating Fact From Popular Fiction

The Millennium: Shocking Facts About a Misunderstood
Prophecy and Your Eternal Destiny

The Rapture Deception

The Truth About the Sabbath

Solving the Mystery of Death

Will My Pet Go to Heaven?

"Thus says the LORD:

'Let not the wise man glory in his wisdom,

Let not the mighty man glory in his might,

Nor let the rich man glory in his riches;

But let him who glories glory in this,

That he understands and knows Me,

That I am the LORD, exercising lovingkindness,

judgment, and righteousness in the earth.

For in these I delight,' says the LORD."

—Jeremiah 9:23, 24

CONTENTS

FOREWORD

There can be no question to the student of the Bible that God is love. Both nature and revelation testify to it. God's love is written on every opening bud and every spire of springing grass (SC 9, 10). God's very nature is to love. But He has other qualities as well, such as wisdom, understanding, power, justice, and mercy. Actually, the divine quality that is spoken of most frequently in the Bible is God's holiness. In fact, the word *holy* appears twice as often there as does the word *love*.

The fact that God is holy is of special interest to the heavenly host. Both the Old and New Testaments record that the angels that are close to God repeat "holy, holy, holy" when they are in His presence (see Isaiah 6:3; Revelation 4:8). It seems that God's love and His holiness are complementary to each other. God can be as loving as He is only because He is holy.

When we develop our mental images of God we tend to see Jesus as the One who held the children and blessed them and who calmed the sea and saved the disciples. We contrast with this image "the vengeful God" who hates sin and destroys sinners. This is one of the main reasons that some people say they are New Testament Christians and leave the Old Testament to those who are still "under the law." From this perspective it is easy to focus on God's love and minimize His holiness. As a result there are those who claim that because of His love, God doesn't kill or directly punish evil. All death, they say, is the result of the natural consequences of sin.

In this important book, Steve Wohlberg and Dr. Chris Lewis take a careful overview of the character of God in both the Old and New Testaments. I believe this balanced and well-researched book will reveal that the authors have done their homework, as evidenced by the careful documentation of their sources. It appears to me that they have approached the subject with an open mind—as much as it is possible to do so—and given readers a good overview of God's essential attributes.

Readers of this book will become aware that God is love but He hates sin and that there is a proper way to hold these two realities in tension. You will discover that God's wrath is not a counterpoint to His love but rather an expression of it. Could it be that God hates sin less because it offends His nature (though it is true that holiness and sin cannot coexist) than because it distorts our perceptions and separates those He loves from Him? If we truly believe that God not only loves but also is love, then we must also believe that He takes no action that is not motivated by love.

Let me add to the illustrations contained in this book. One of Satan's strategies in his deception of Eve was to undermine the reality of God's judgment. He told her, " 'You will not surely die' " (Genesis 3:4). But he set the stage for this deception by first trying to get Eve to doubt God's love through asking, " 'Has God indeed said, "You shall not eat of every tree of the garden"?' " (verse 1). Satan's strategy worked on Eve, and it works on many today. Our sin is rooted, not only in a lack of reverence for God's holiness, but also in a woefully insufficient understanding of His love.

In the final analysis, God's destruction of the wicked is an act of love for His people and of mercy toward the wicked. "Could those whose hearts are filled with hatred of God, of truth and holiness, mingle with the heavenly throng and join their songs of praise? Could they endure the glory of God and the Lamb? No, no; years of probation were granted them, that they might form characters for heaven; but they have never trained the mind to love purity; they have never learned the language of heaven, and now it is too late. A life of rebellion against God has unfitted them for heaven. Its purity, holiness, and peace would be torture to them; the glory of God would be a consuming fire. They would long to flee from that holy place. They would welcome destruction, that they might be hidden from the face of Him who died to redeem them. The destiny of the wicked is fixed by their own choice. Their exclusion from heaven is voluntary with themselves, and just and merciful on the part of God" (GC 542, 543).

So instead of saying "God is love, but He also hates sin," we could more correctly say, "God is love, *and this is why He hates sin.*" We are all part of a great love story—the plan of salvation—and what we all need desperately is to know our God better. This book gives us a better understanding of His love.

G. Edward Reid

INTRODUCTION

Under the heading "Google Zeitgeist," the December 31, 2007, edition of *Time* magazine posted a "year-end report on the fastest-rising and most popular searches on Google." After noting that among the top draws were *American Idol,* Ron Paul, and Anna Nicole Smith, the report declared, "Some of life's bigger questions were also search-engine staples." Significantly, one of the most popular questions Internet surfers sought information about was who God is.[1]

This book is about the answer to that question. Specifically, it's about who God is *on the inside*—that is, the nature of His character. This is definitely one of "life's bigger questions" (quoting *Time*); one that captivates countless human beings both inside and outside of Christianity. The query "What is God like?" is intensely controversial within the church of which Dr. Chris Lewis and I are members—the Seventh-day Adventist Church. But Adventists aren't alone in their struggle to discern God's heart correctly. Baptists, Methodists, Lutherans, Catholics, and Pentecostals wrestle with this too. So do Jews, Muslims, and Wiccans. So do agnostics. Truly, the question "Who is God?" is of universal concern. It's important to everyone.

According to the Bible, this question is also a matter of life and death. Jesus Christ declared, " 'This is eternal life, that they may know You, the only true God, and Jesus Christ whom You have sent' " (John 17:3). Here Jesus stated that truly knowing the Father and His Son means "eternal life." Conversely, not knowing Them can easily become the route to damnation. " ' "I never knew you," ' " Jesus will someday sadly announce to a group of misguided people, " ' "depart from Me" ' " (Matthew 7:23). These Scriptures should impress us with the necessity of knowing God "as He is" (1 John 3:2) instead of only as we think He is.

The danger of deception is real and should be taken seriously. The Bible's last book solemnly warns about "that serpent of old, called the Devil and Satan, *who deceives the whole world*" (Revelation 12:9; emphasis added). So, in our quest to know God aright, we should beware of the serpent's wiles. Ignorance of his cunning and activity is not bliss. Instead, it's potentially deadly. Life is not a game. Our souls are at stake. We should never forget that our enemy has thousands of years of experience in twisting truth, and that in these last days, his infernal goal is to " 'deceive, if possible, even the elect' " (Matthew 24:24). Thus we must be on our guard, just as certainly as American soldiers must beware of al-Qaida.

Especially should we beware of satanic imbalances. Church history is littered with extremism propagated by those claiming to be God's holiest representatives. During the so-called Dark Ages, countless murders were committed in the name of the Lord. Bloody crusades were launched, innocent children were slaughtered, and torture chambers were established beneath apparently sacred monasteries. Did black-hooded inquisitors represent God correctly? We think not. Still others, while they didn't torture anyone, advanced such harsh views of God's wrath and justice that people have imagined the Supreme Being to be nothing more than a heartless, loveless monster in the sky. All such extremism and religious barbarism only fuel the cause of atheism, for who would want to spend eternity with a god like that?

But there are other extremes equally as dangerous. On the opposite side of the fence are the many Christian pastors and teachers who have taught—and who still teach today—that God is so friendly, so gentlemanly, and so nice that fallen human beings can get away with practically anything. Such teachers rarely emphasize the seriousness of sin, the reality of divine justice, or retribution that breaking the Ten Commandments will eventually bring. Especially do they resist or ignore the idea that God hates evil. "How can a loving God hate anything?" they question.

In the chapters that follow, we will examine closely a particular perspective that is gaining momentum in the Adventist Church, yet the issues apply to everyone. While there are some variations, the general idea is that, yes, sin exists and it will receive justice, but God doesn't punish evil directly, for doing so would be contrary to His character of love—He just "isn't that kind of person." In essence, according to this view, sin punishes itself, or Satan does the punishing just as soon as God removes His protective hand.

While we recognize that sin does carry built-in consequences, that the devil is a heartless murderer, and that the Lord often does indeed withdraw His protection from those who persistently spurn Him, the questions are: Does this mean that the God-doesn't-kill theory has revealed the full picture? What is the nature of God's justice? What about His wrath? How can His wrath be reconciled with His love, especially with the tender love that Jesus Christ revealed? Above all, what does the agony of our Savior in the Garden of Gethsemane and on the cross teach us about the relationship between God's mercy and His justice? We will investigate each of these vital questions closely in the following pages.

A few clarifications

As we begin this controversial, emotional journey, Dr. Lewis and I wish to clarify a few things.* First, our primary source of authority is the Bible, which has been "given by inspiration of God, . . . for doctrine, for reproof, for correction, for instruction in righteousness" (2 Timothy 3:16). We firmly accept the Protestant principle that the Bible *alone* is the foundation of all true doctrine and the basis of all correct teaching. Yet we have also been blessed by the spiritual insights of another writer, who, remarkably, is the most widely translated female author in the history of literature: Ellen G. White. We have prayerfully chosen to include select quotes from her pen too. But again, this book is based on the Bible, not her writings, and we will use all extra-biblical quotations only to support and emphasize what Scripture says.

We also realize that not everyone will agree with our conclusions. If you don't, we hope you won't consider us your enemies. This is not our view of those who believe differently than we do. We, as you, seek to honor Jesus Christ and to know Him aright. Jesus told us to " 'love one another' "

---

* Please note that while Dr. Lewis and I use the first-person plural in this introduction, for ease of reading, the rest of this book has been written primarily in the first-person singular, from Steve Wohlberg's perspective, though Dr. Lewis has truly been a coauthor too.

(John 13:34), and this is what we should do even when we disagree.

We recognize that not everyone believes exactly the same thing; thus in the following pages, we have tried our best to represent correctly, without mentioning the names of the proponents, what we consider to be a growing trend within our church. We have sought to be fair. If in any way we have failed, forgive us. As spirited dialogue will surely result from what we've written here, we hope to be treated fairly too. The fact is that we all have one primary enemy—one whose Greek name means "the adversary." May we all detect and resist his subversive and intensely personal hostility to truth.

Now for a disclaimer: This book is not an exhaustive study of God's character, and it can't possibly examine every Bible text about His love, mercy, wrath, and justice. No book can do that; further exploration will always be needed. In fact, those who enter the heavenly kingdom will ponder God's goodness throughout eternity, and there will always be more to learn. Yet we believe that the scriptures used here, the explanations offered, and the broad principles covered should be more than sufficient to answer the basic question, What is God like? We also hope to expose many of Lucifer's subtle distortions, which he has carefully crafted to cloud our understanding of the true attributes of the King of the kings and to pervert His plan of salvation.

One more observation: Dr. Lewis's and my ultimate goal in coauthoring *The Character of God Controversy* isn't theoretical, academic, or cerebral. Far from it. Neither is it to generate conflict or division, although sometimes these can't be avoided. Our greatest desire is to reveal the incredible love and incomprehensible pain of a Father and His Son, and we hope to do this so powerfully that you will be forever changed.

Dr. Lewis and I both have children. As is true of most parents, words cannot describe our commitment to our kids. We aren't lying when we say we would willingly die for them. Being separated from them is unthinkable. Well, the unthinkable happened nearly two thousand years ago just outside Jerusalem on a lonely hill called "Place of a Skull" (Matthew 27:33). Mercy and justice grasped hands, kissed, and wept. When Jesus cried, " 'My God, My God, why have You forsaken Me?' " (verse 46) and then finally, " 'It is finished!' " (John 19:30), billions of holy intelligences heard what He said and understood as never before the heart of God. At the same moment, innumerable demons, driven by sheer desperation, renewed their commitment to distort the truth as long as time should last.

Ellen White wrote, "It is Satan's constant effort to misrepresent the character of God, the nature of sin, and the real issues at stake in the great controversy" (GC 569). Our hope is that this book will enable you to detect these misrepresentations and discern the real issues at stake, and that it will inspire you to take your stand firmly on the side of " 'the only true God, and Jesus Christ whom [He has] sent' " (John 17:3). Soon the great controversy between our loving Creator and His evil enemy will be forever ended. May we all enjoy eternity with the One who died for us.

Dear Lord, open our eyes, reveal Yourself, and teach us Your truth. In Jesus Christ's name. Amen.

---

1. "Google Zeitgeist," *Time*, December 31, 2007, 31.

CHAPTER 1

WAR ZONE

When a thing ceases to be a subject of controversy,
it ceases to be a subject of interest.

—William Hazlitt

"And war broke out in heaven" (Revelation 12:7). This verse takes us back to phase one of an intense conflict that has been raging for thousands of years, yet is soon to close. "Michael and his angels fought with the dragon; and the dragon and his angels fought" (verse 7). In a faraway realm beyond the stars, "the dragon" and his cohorts engaged in some sort of active, desperate combat against "Michael" and the loyal angels and were defeated. "So the great dragon was cast out, that serpent of old, called the Devil and Satan, who deceives the whole world; he was cast to the earth, and his angels were cast out with him" (verse 9).

A careful analysis of Revelation 12:7–9 reveals many things. First, it communicates that we are in a war. The Greek word translated "war" in verse 7 is *polemos*. This word occurs eighteen times in the New Testament. The King James Version translates *polemos* as "war" twelve times, as "battle" five times, and as "fight" once. Strong's concordance defines *polemos* as (1) a war; (2) a fight, a battle; or (3) a dispute, strife, or quarrel.[1]

Most significantly, the eye of the storm in this war/fight/battle/dispute/strife/quarrel is the person of God Himself. We can discover this by looking closely at the name of the one who fought the dragon, *Michael*. Strong's concordance states that the name *Michael* means "Who is like God."[2] Thus it is God and what He is like that was the center of the conflict. And it all started when Lucifer—a.k.a. "the dragon . . . the Devil and Satan"—the instigator of the great war, inappropriately aspired to become "like God." Isaiah reported,

"How you are fallen from heaven,
O Lucifer, son of the morning!
How you are cut down to the ground,
You who weakened the nations!
For you have said in your heart:
'I will ascend into heaven,
I will exalt my throne above the stars of God;
I will also sit on the mount of the congregation
On the farthest sides of the north;
I will ascend above the heights of the clouds,
I will be like the Most High' " (Isaiah 14:12–14).

Lucifer wanted to "be like the Most High." This doesn't mean that he wanted to reflect God's kindness. Instead, he wanted to rule, to govern, to direct the heavenly host *in the Lord's place*. A little reflection will teach us that the reason for his perverse aspirations must have been that somehow, mysteriously, he had first lost confidence in his Maker. Exactly how this happened no one knows for sure. It is part of the mystery of iniquity.

Lucifer's " 'heart was lifted up' " (Ezekiel 28:17). As his heart became proud, doubts about God arose too. Inside his formerly perfect, angelic head there developed "a strange, fierce conflict" (PP 37). Previously, Lucifer had trusted completely in the love, wisdom, and justice of his Creator, but not anymore. Now he questioned his Maker's goodness. In other words, he questioned the Lord's character. Such questioning is the only logical reason why he then decided to seek to usurp God's position as the recognized Sovereign of the universe. Notice carefully these three successive steps: (1) Lucifer's heart became proud, (2) next he questioned God's character, and (3) then he wanted to take God's place.

"He deceived angels"

The devil wasn't satisfied to meander down this rocky road alone. In the course of his rebellion against his Maker, this mighty angel chose to actively instill his own subversive doubts into the hearts of his angelic comrades. Notice these insightful comments: "Sin originated in self-seeking. Lucifer, the covering cherub, desired to be first in heaven. He sought to gain control of heavenly beings, to draw them away from their Creator, and to win their homage to himself. Therefore he misrepresented God, attributing to Him the desire for self-exaltation. With his own evil characteristics he sought to invest the loving Creator. Thus he deceived angels" (DA 21, 22).

Don't miss the significant sequence: "He misrepresented God. . . . Thus he deceived angels" (ibid.). So, misrepresenting God was Satan's primary method of seducing holy angels. His plan worked with deadly effectiveness. Somehow, a vast host of previously perfect beings believed his lies. Eventually, permanent lines were drawn, and a cosmic war erupted. This is why "the great dragon was cast out, that serpent of old, called the Devil and Satan, who deceives the whole world; he was cast to the earth, and his angels were cast out with him" (Revelation 12:9).

Revelation 12:9 informs us that the prince of darkness not only deceived heavenly angels, but that he "deceives the whole world." Think about it. If Satan's main method of deceiving angels was to misrepresent God's character, doesn't it make sense that he would use the same tactic to mislead human beings? No doubt. And if this method was successful against flawless angels, how easily it works against fallen men! "Therefore [Lucifer] misrepresented God. . . . Thus he deceived angels. *Thus he deceived men*" (DA 21, 22; emphasis added).

There you have it. In heaven, Satan first became proud. As a by-product of his pride, he questioned God's character. Not satisfied to keep his doubts private, he then deliberately began the artful work of misrepresenting God to his holy friends. "Thus he deceived angels." Ever since the fall of Adam and Eve (see Genesis 3), he has been following the same plan. *Thus he deceives men.* Therefore, the root issue in the great controversy between God and the devil concerns the character of the King of the universe. What is He really like? What is He like on the inside? Within the deepest depths of His mysterious personality, is the Maker of everything really loving, just, fair, and true? Or was Lucifer right? This is the radio-active central issue in the war in which we are now engaged.

This conflict over the person of God has continued throughout human history inside the hearts and minds of human beings among every nation and within every culture. It raged throughout ancient Egypt, Assyria, Babylon, Persia, Greece, and Rome. Through Satan's machinations, "the earth was dark through misapprehension of God" (DA 22). Even in the land of the Jews, his deceptions were successful. Many of God's own chosen people had warped perceptions about the One who rules in the heavens.

"Whose minds the god of this age [had] blinded" (2 Corinthians 4:4). Duped by the enemy, they desperately needed enlightenment.

"That the gloomy shadows might be lightened, that the world might be brought back to God, Satan's deceptive power was to be broken" (DA 22).

Who could accomplish such a feat? Who could successfully shatter Satan's delusions? Only one Person—Jesus Christ. "This work only one Being in all the universe could do. Only He who knew the height and depth of the love of God could make it known. Upon the world's dark night the Sun of Righteousness must rise, 'with healing in His wings.' Mal. 4:2" (ibid.).

Leaving the indescribable glories of a much brighter land than we've ever seen, Jesus entered our dark world to counteract Satan's falsehoods. *His primary strategy was to reveal God's loving character to humanity.* Misguided men and desperate demons fought Him at every step. The battle was intense. Nevertheless, Christ accomplished His holy mission. Near the end of His earthly life He boldly informed Philip, " 'He who has seen Me has seen the Father' " (John 14:9). Yes indeed! Jesus revealed His Father's character perfectly, wonderfully, and magnificently, without a trace of imperfection. He was "the brightness of His [Father's] glory and the express image of His person" (Hebrews 1:3). Because of this flawless revelation and because of the great love that constantly flowed through Him, many Jews and Gentiles surrendered their hearts to their Maker, joining the ranks of holy angels who never fell.

In the time of the end

Two thousand years have come and gone since Jesus Christ walked this earth. " 'The time of the end' " (Daniel 12:4) has arrived. To the discerning, the signs of the times are obvious and ominous. Hollywood immorality, Wall Street uncertainty, domestic violence, natural disasters, Islamic terrorism, and senseless school shootings confront and sicken us on every side. Our world is in trouble—big time. The Spirit of God is withdrawing from the hearts and minds of human beings. Yet in the midst of global chaos, earth's Maker still speaks. He knocks, convicts, woos, and appeals. " 'Come to Me,' " Jesus pleads, " 'and I will give you rest' " (Matthew 11:28).

Thank God, there's still hope. The sixtieth chapter of Isaiah contains a wonderful prophecy about the rising of special light at the very time that earth's darkness is the deepest. Isaiah wrote,

"Arise, shine;
For your light has come!
And the glory of the Lord *is risen upon you.*
For behold, the darkness shall cover the earth,
And deep darkness the people;
But the Lord will arise over you,
And His glory will be seen upon you"
(Isaiah 60:1, 2; emphasis added).

Another verse in the same book predicts,
"The glory of the Lord shall be revealed,

> *And all flesh shall see it together;*
> *For the mouth of the* Lord *has spoken"* (Isaiah 40:5; emphasis added).

These verses tell us that at the exact time that "darkness shall cover the earth, and deep darkness the people," something magnificent will occur. "The glory of the Lord shall be revealed," the glory of the Lord will rise, and "His glory will be seen" upon His people. This is the Word of God. It will happen, "for the mouth of the Lord has spoken" it.

What is the glory of the Lord? We don't need to speculate, because the same Bible that makes the prediction explains the mystery. Standing upon the summit of Mount Sinai, Moses requested of the Lord, " 'Please, show me Your glory' " (Exodus 33:18). Notice carefully the divine response. "The Lord said, 'Here is a place by Me, and you shall stand on the rock. So it shall be, while My glory passes by, that I will put you in the cleft of the rock, and will cover you with My hand while I pass by' " (Exodus 33:21, 22). So, God told Moses that His glory would pass before him. Seven verses later there's a description of what happened. The Lord "passed before him" (Exodus 34:6). Then what did God do? *He revealed the attributes of His character!* See Exodus 34:6, 7. (We will carefully examine those attributes in the next chapter of this book.) By comparing Exodus 33:18–22, where Moses asked to see God's "glory," with Exodus 34:5–7, where the Lord answered his request, we discover that God's glory is His character. And by linking these texts with the prophecies in Isaiah 40:5 and 60:1, 2, we learn that it is the light of His character that is to illuminate what the Bible calls the darkness of this world. This darkness can't be referring to mere air pollution. Instead, it refers to a satanically inspired mental blindness that enshrouds most people's thinking about what God is really like.

> It is the darkness of misapprehension of God that is enshrouding the world. Men are losing their knowledge of His character. It has been misunderstood and misinterpreted. At this time a message from God is to be proclaimed, a message illuminating in its influence and saving in its power. His character is to be made known. Into the darkness of the world is to be shed the light of His glory, the light of His goodness, mercy, and truth.
>
> This is the work outlined by the prophet Isaiah in the words, "O Jerusalem, that bringest good tidings, lift up thy voice with strength; lift it up, be not afraid; say unto the cities of Judah, Behold your God! Behold, the Lord God will come with strong hand, and His arm shall rule for Him; behold, his reward is with Him, and His work before Him." Isaiah 40:9, 10.
>
> Those who wait for the Bridegroom's coming are to say to the people, "Behold your God." The last rays of merciful light, the last message of mercy to be given to the world, is a revelation of His character of love (COL 415).

A message from God

"Behold your God!" This is the climactic appeal of Isaiah the prophet. We need to behold our Maker as He really is, to discern His character. But don't forget that there's a war going on. It began in heaven and will rage until the close of time. The first paragraph that we've quoted from *Christ's Object Lessons* informs us that God's character "has been misunderstood and misinterpreted." Lucifer and his legions, masters of misinformation, are behind all such distortions, and their activity is the root cause of the moral darkness now "enshrouding the world." Yet in these last days, at this very moment, according to multiple predictions in the book of Isaiah, "a message from God is to be proclaimed, a message illuminating in its influence and saving in its power. *His character is to be made known.* Into the darkness of the world is to be shed the light of His glory, the light of His goodness, mercy, and truth" (emphasis added).

Don't miss that last word in the sentence above. Heaven's special light, which is "the light of His glory," is also "the light of His mercy, goodness, and *truth*" (emphasis added). We human beings need truth without error. And based on the research we did before we wrote this book, it is the truth about God that is the eye of the storm. This truth is the center of the war we're engaged in. Our enemy hates this truth, and he will resist it with furious intensity because " 'there is no truth in him' " (John 8:44). Yet his plotting is doomed to fail. Despite his hellish efforts, God's end-time people will someday arise, shine, and reveal God's glory. The Lord's message will be given.

Again, "the last rays of merciful light, the last message of mercy to be given to the world, is a revelation of His character of love." Those "last rays of merciful light" are shining now. May we fully receive them before it's too late.

---

1. James Strong, *The Exhaustive Concordance of the Bible: Showing Every Word of the Text of the Common English Version of the Canonical Books, and Every Occurrence of Each Word in Regular Order*, electronic edition (Elmira, Ontario: Woodside Bible Fellowship, 1996), s.v. "polemos."
2. Ibid., s.v. "Michael."

For Further Thought and Discussion

1. What do we know about Lucifer before he fell?
2. What important lessons can we learn as we study the tragic history of Lucifer's rebellion against his Maker?
3. What can we learn about God's character from His response to Lucifer's rebellion?
4. Why is correctly understanding what God is like so important?
5. What are some popular yet dangerous misconceptions about God's character, and what are the negative consequences of believing them?
6. Where does the Bible teach that God's end-time people are called to reflect His character to the world?
7. Why is reflecting God's character so important today?
8. Describe what God's people would be like if they truly revealed His character in these last days.
9. What impressed you the most in this chapter, and why?

CHAPTER 2

CLEFT OF THE ROCK CLARITY

Now Mount Sinai was completely in smoke, because the LORD descended upon it in fire. Its smoke ascended like the smoke of a furnace, and the whole mountain quaked greatly.

—Exodus 19:18

Can you imagine what it must have been like for Moses to hike up Mount Sinai? I have trekked up many steep slopes in the High Sierras of northern California, but I've never seen anything like what the text above describes. The gullies and ridges of Mount Sinai literally rocked back and forth as the Almighty descended upon the mountain. Blazing fire engulfed the mountain's summit, and the ascending smoke was visible for miles. Never before in recorded human history had the Lord appeared with such fireworks. Two significant events were slated to occur: God was about to engrave the Ten Commandments with His own finger on solid stone, and He was to audibly state the attributes of His character.

The Lord told Moses, " 'Be ready in the morning, and come up in the morning to Mount Sinai, and present yourself to Me there on the top of the mountain' " (Exodus 34:2). Moses obeyed, hiked up that rugged hill, presented himself before God, and then waited with bated breath. Suddenly a bright cloud descended upon the top of the mountain, and a holy hand reached out from within its sacred mist. The hand then literally lifted this special man off his feet and gently placed him in a " 'cleft of the rock' " (Exodus 33:22).

"Now the LORD descended in the cloud and stood with him there, and proclaimed the name of the LORD. And the LORD passed before him and proclaimed, 'The LORD, the LORD God, merciful and gracious, long-suffering, and abounding in goodness and truth, keeping mercy for thousands, forgiving iniquity and transgression and sin, by no means clearing the guilty, visiting the iniquity of the fathers upon the children and the children's children to the third and the fourth generation' " (Exodus 34:5–7).

There it is, the most complete, *verbal* revelation of God's character ever given in the history of the universe to that time, and it was "proclaimed" by the Lord Himself to His sheltered servant. Awed by the deep significance of the revelation, "Moses made haste and bowed his head toward the earth, and worshiped" (Exodus 34:8).

It's one thing for humans to talk about what they *think* God is like, and another thing entirely for the Lord Himself to state His own attributes. Lucifer certainly has his opinions, which he covertly expressed to shining angels before both he and they were evicted from their heavenly home. The world's religions have their theories too—theories often secretly inspired by the fallen foe.

In the midst of global confusion, we need the truth. And God plainly revealed that truth when He passed by Moses.

God's true character

Exodus 34:5–7 proves that God's true character is a perfect blend of various attributes. The Ruler of the universe is

- "merciful,"
- "gracious,"
- "longsuffering,"
- "abounding in goodness and truth,"
- "keeping mercy for thousands,"
- "forgiving iniquity and transgression and sin,"
- "by no means clearing the guilty,"
- "visiting the iniquity of the fathers upon the children and the children's children to the third and the fourth generation."

Just as tasty cuisine results from a masterful combination of different foods, condiments, and seasonings, even so does Exodus 34:5–7 reveal God's character to be a perfect blend of various attributes. Like Joseph's coat of many colors, our Maker's heart has diverse shades and textures. It is a rich tapestry. "Merciful and gracious, longsuffering, and . . . forgiving" are exquisitely mixed with "abounding in goodness and truth." Then additional seasoning is added: "by no means clearing the guilty."

Essentially, we see graciousness, mercy, and patience mixed with holiness and justice. The fact that God abounds in "goodness" reveals that He is inherently good, *not evil.* "Forgiving iniquity and transgression and sin" reveals not only His absolute morality, but also His desire to pardon those who offend against His government. To God, "iniquity and transgression and sin" surely exist, and to Him, they are utterly repulsive; yet He is still kind and forgiving. Truly, God is an infinite Personality, never fully fathomable by any creature. Yet we must try. We must explore His apparent contradictions to the best of our ability. That is the purpose of this book.

Notice the following significant quotations about the importance of Exodus 34:5–7.

> It was to Moses that God revealed His glory in those wonderful words that have been the treasured heritage of the ages: "The Lord, the Lord God, merciful and gracious, long-suffering, and abundant in goodness and truth, keeping mercy for thousands, forgiving iniquity and transgression and sin." Exodus 34:6, 7 (MB 46).

> [Moses] saw mercy and justice blended in harmony and love expressed without a parallel (ST, June 17, 1880).

> We are called to represent to the world the character of God as it was revealed to Moses (6T 221).

These are powerful statements. Not only does Exodus 34:5–7 contain God's self-revelation, but it is "the treasured heritage of the ages" and describes the very attributes "we are called to represent to the world."

Now here's a key question: Where was Jesus Christ when Moses crouched inside that "cleft of the rock"? Was He there at all? Was it His character that was proclaimed to Moses, or that of Another? These are highly controversial questions, with large implications. Many Christians today see a sharp contrast between the God of the Old Testament and the God of the New Testament. To them, it's Jehovah versus Jesus Christ. Jehovah is often pictured as stern and harsh, while Jesus is seen as meek and mild. *Give me Jesus, not the God of Mount Sinai!* is the sentiment of many hearts. So, whose character did Moses hear described?

He existed before His birth

The Bible has the answer. First of all, our Savior's existence didn't begin in Bethlehem. Micah had predicted,

> "But you, Bethlehem Ephrathah,
> Though you are little among the thousands of Judah,
> Yet out of you shall come forth to Me
> The One to be Ruler in Israel,
> Whose goings forth are from of old,
> From everlasting" (Micah 5:2).

Israel's Messiah has existed "from everlasting." He was living long before lowly shepherds heard angels sing near Bethlehem. In fact, the New Testament clearly says that the Son of God was with His Father at the creation of the world. Calling Christ "the Word," John's Gospel reports, "In the beginning was the Word, and the Word was with God, and the Word was God. He was in the beginning with God. *All things were made through Him,* and without Him nothing was made that was made" (John 1:1–3; emphasis added).

The Bible says that the Father created our earth *through* His Son. Before becoming the Babe of Bethlehem, Jesus was the active Agent of Creation. Paul testified, "God . . . created all things by Jesus Christ" (Ephesians 3:9, KJV). At the beginning of the world, the words " 'Let Us make man in Our image' " (Genesis 1:26) were exchanged between the Father and the Son. They were the "Us." During the forty years of wilderness wandering after the Exodus, the Israelites "drank of that spiritual Rock that followed them, *and that Rock was Christ*" (1 Corinthians 10:4; emphasis added). So it was Jesus Himself who journeyed with Israel in the wilderness.

Who was it, then, who gave the Ten Commandments to Moses on Mount Sinai? Specifically, who passed before Moses, revealing His character? Here's the answer:

After Israel had been in bondage in Egypt . . . the Lord led them

forth into the wilderness. He had them assemble about Mount
Sinai, and there, amid awful grandeur, *Jesus Christ,* who was the
founder of the whole Jewish economy, *spoke the ten precepts* of God
to the people (ST, March 12, 1894; emphasis added).

> *By Christ the law was proclaimed from Sinai* (ST, September
> 14, 1882; emphasis added).

> His clear, ringing voice—*the same that upon Mount Sinai pro-
> claimed the law* that priests and rulers are transgressing—is heard
> echoing through the arches of the temple: "Take these things
> hence; make not My Father's house an house of merchandise"
> (DA 158; emphasis added).

So, Jesus Christ created our world, led Israel to Mount Sinai, gave the
Ten Commandments, and later—as a Man—cleansed the unholy traffic
from the Jewish temple. In fact, "after the transgression of Adam, the
Lord spoke no longer directly with man; the human race was given into
the hands of Christ, and *all communication came through Him to the
world*" (FCE 237; emphasis added). Thus it was definitely the hand of
our Lord Jesus Christ that hid Moses in the "cleft of the rock" before His
own glory passed by. It can be no other way. Fourteen hundred years
later, that same hand was nailed to a cross.

The pervasive Old Testament God versus New Testament Jesus dichotomy taught in so many churches, even by many so-called Bible
scholars, is completely unbiblical. Remember, when Jesus was on earth,
He informed Philip, " 'He who has seen Me has seen the Father' " (John
14:9). This means not only that Jesus revealed His Father's character *but
that their divine attributes are the same.* It's incorrect to state, "The God
of the Old Testament is bad, but Jesus is good." Such reasoning is false.
It isn't true that our heavenly Father is mean, but Jesus is friendly. Such
thinking not only perverts the Scriptures but also inadvertently seconds
the opinion of Lucifer that Someone above is faulty. That was his original
line, which holy angels fell for. Don't you be deceived.

Moses declared, " 'Hear, O Israel: The LORD our God, the LORD is
one! " (Deuteronomy 6:4; emphasis added). There aren't two Gods in
heaven, there's only One. Yet the Hebrew word translated "God" is *elo-*

him, which is actually a plural term. The same word is used in Genesis 1:26, which says, "Then God [*elohim,* plural] said, 'Let Us make man in Our image.' " Thus God is an "Us." So how can "Us" be One? The simple answer is that the Father, Son, and Holy Spirit are perfectly united and have *identical* character qualities. They are never at odds with each Other— never. One isn't gentle and nice, while the other is rough and harsh. No. Their attributes are the same. Thus "the LORD is one!"

Diversity within the divine character

Now don't miss this point: although there is no diversity between the Father, Son, and Holy Spirit, there *is* diversity within their divine attributes. Moses clearly discerned this diversity as he peeked through a crack between holy fingers attached to a holy hand that gently covered the "cleft of the rock" where he lay hidden. "Merciful," God proclaimed, and this was followed by "abounding in goodness and truth." But then came "by no means clearing the guilty, visiting the iniquity of the fathers upon the children." These are *diverse* attributes within *one* character. It should be obvious that "merciful" is not exactly the same as "visiting the iniquity." Mercy is not justice, and justice is not mercy. Ask any police officer who issues you a speeding ticket. Ask the judge when you appear in traffic court. If you get mercy, you're off the hook; if you receive justice, you pay a fine. *They're not the same.*

Not everyone will accept or believe what they read in this book. But remember, there's an intense controversy raging over the character of God. In the midst of many views, heated emotions, and demonic notions, it is our task to discern the truth. How can we do this? The only way is for us to hide ourselves in the "cleft of the rock" and let God teach us. The Lord Himself is the only One who can truly reveal His character to us, and He does it through the Bible. We must humbly accept what He shows us.

Ultimately, discerning God's true character is a deeply spiritual issue. Take a look: "Selfishness prevents us from beholding God. The self-seeking spirit judges of God as altogether such a one as itself. Until we have renounced this, we cannot understand Him who is love. Only the unselfish heart, the humble and trustful spirit, shall see God as 'merciful and gracious, long-suffering, and abundant in goodness and truth' " (DA 302).

Did you catch that? It is "only the unselfish heart, the humble and trustful spirit" that *can* "see God" as He truly is. Remember, Lucifer first became proud and then he starting viewing God *as He wasn't*—that is, as "altogether such a one as [himself]." The real problem wasn't the Lord at all, but Lucifer. Therefore, if we are ever to overcome Satan's spirit and thoughts, we must begin where he failed—with humility. Until we have renounced both pride and selfishness, "we cannot understand Him who is love."

On the top of Mount Sinai, because of his "humble and trustful spirit," Moses saw God aright, and the revelation filled him with wonder. When he finally descended the rugged slope, it was obvious that something highly unusual had occurred. Moses was different. Not just spiritually, mentally, and emotionally, but even physically. Amazingly, his face literally glowed with a heavenly brightness. The Word reports, "So when Aaron and all the children of Israel saw Moses, behold, the skin of his face shone, and they were afraid to come near him" (Exodus 34:30). Moses was now the man with the shiny face. "The impress of God was upon him, making him appear as one of the shining angels from the throne" (4T 533).

At the summit of a smoking mountain, as he crouched low in that "cleft of a rock," Moses discerned God's character with its blended elements of mercy and justice. Even more than this, he saw the gospel, which we will zero in on soon. And what he saw made his face glow.

Lucifer must have cringed.

For Further Thought and Discussion

1. Why is Exodus 34:5–8 such an important Bible passage?
2. Discuss the meaning and significance of each divine attribute revealed in Exodus 34:6, 7.
3. Give some examples from the Old Testament in which God manifested some of these attributes.
4. Give some examples from the New Testament in which Jesus Christ revealed some of these same attributes.
5. Why is it so important that we understand that Jesus Christ and His Father are One in character?
6. Why is it so important that we correctly understand the Lord's mercy?
7. Why is it so important that we correctly understand His justice?
8. What is the relationship between the spiritual condition of our hearts and our ability to discern God's heart correctly?
9. What impressed you the most in this chapter, and why?

CHAPTER 3

LOYAL LEVITES AND THE GOLDEN CALF

Moderation in the pursuit of justice is no virtue.

—Barry Goldwater

Sixteen fierce wildfires fueled by gusty Santa Ana winds devastated much of Southern California in October 2007. My family didn't just read about them; we saw the smoke. On Tuesday, October 23, my wife, Kristin, three-year-old son, Seth, and I meandered around the hot spots in our minivan on Interstates 10, 210, and 5 as we journeyed from Palm Springs toward Fresno. Reddish haze confronted our eyes on every side. We saw large trucks that had been knocked over by the wind. At least fifteen hundred homes were reduced to ashes by unquenchable flames, with nine fatalities. The blazes were intense, destructive, and terrible. Those who lived through that nightmare will never forget it.

In these last days of earth's history, the subject of the justice of God and especially of the reality and nature of His wrath is hot as well. It definitely generates heated emotions, and it often polarizes. "God is love" the Bible informs us (1 John 4:8). While hidden in that " 'cleft of the rock' " (Exodus 33: 21), Moses saw that the Maker of planet Earth is merciful, gracious, patient, and forgiving. But what about the justice part of His character? Is God's justice active (carried out by Him), passive (something He allows others to do), or both? Even more importantly, is God's justice *just*? In this chapter we will begin to tackle this tough topic. Our goal is to examine it fairly, intelligently, and biblically. Above all, we wish to see the relationship between God's justice and His love, for it is "a revelation of His character of love" (COL 415) that must now be given to the world. The full answer to these vital questions will come in later chapters.

As we've already seen, Exodus 34:5–7 contains God's own description of His character. After highlighting His graciousness, mercy, and forgiveness, the Lord Almighty also declared, " 'by no means clearing the guilty, visiting the iniquity of the fathers upon the children and the children's children to the third and the fourth generation' " (verse 7). This latter part of the description reveals His justice—that is, how He relates to the guilty. Of particular interest is the statement about His "visiting the iniquity" or punishing sin. What does this mean?

Some interpret "visiting the iniquity" to mean that God simply allows natural consequences to run their course. In other words, according to this perspective, God doesn't personally or directly punish transgression. Rather, He merely permits cause-and-effect consequences to occur. There is some truth to this, for sin surely has natural consequences. Notice these comments on "visiting the iniquity":

> "Visiting the iniquity of the fathers upon the children unto the third and fourth generation of them that hate Me." It is inevitable that children should suffer from the consequences of parental wrongdoing, but they are not punished for the parents' guilt, except as they participate in their sins. It is usually the case, however, that children walk in the steps of their parents. By inheritance and example the sons become partakers of the father's sin. Wrong tendencies, perverted appetites, and debased morals, as well as physical disease and degeneracy, are transmitted as a legacy from father to son, to the third and fourth generation. This fearful truth should have a solemn power to restrain men from following a course of sin (PP 306).

This enlightening paragraph stresses the inevitable "consequences of parental wrongdoing," which include transmitting "wrong tendencies, perverted appetites, and debased morals, as well as physical disease and degeneracy" to children. "Like father, like son," is a true saying. If Mom and Dad live reckless, godless, immoral lives, their evil course will naturally affect their offspring, even to the third and fourth generation.

Sin's natural consequences

Yes, there are natural consequences to sin. When God created our world, He established certain fixed laws, the violation of which bring inescapable penalties. There are both natural laws and spiritual laws. There is, for instance, the law of gravity. What goes up comes down. Jump off a cliff without a parachute, and you'll get hurt. There are also health laws. Eat a high-fat diet, and you increase your chances of suffering from obesity, diabetes, and other chronic diseases. Smoking leads to lung cancer and so forth. Then there are laws of the mind. If your children watch lots of violence on TV, they will become prone to violence. Those who view pornography will probably end up acting perversely. By beholding, we become changed. Yes, there are consequences to how we think and what we do. Every seed will produce a corresponding harvest. Paul wrote, "Whatever a man sows, that he will also reap" (Galatians 6:7). It's the truth.

Notice this additional comment about this from generation to generation principle: "Against every transgression of the laws of life, nature will utter her protest. She bears abuse as long as she can; but finally the retribution comes, and it falls upon the mental as well as the physical powers. Nor does it end with the transgressor; the effects of his indulgence are seen in his offspring, and thus the evil is passed down from generation to generation" (CH 112).

So, when God says, "visiting the iniquity of the fathers upon the children and the children's children to the third and the fourth generation," such "visiting" does indeed include natural consequences. The above paragraph even calls such consequences "retribution." But, more importantly, we must ask, Is that it? In other words, does the justice part of God's character merely mean that He permits the natural effects of wrongdoing to run their course, or is He more actively involved?

We don't have to guess. We can discover a definite answer by taking a closer look at the immediate context of Exodus 34:5–7. God had been exceedingly gracious to the descendants of Abraham, Isaac, and Jacob. By awesome acts of supernatural power, He had miraculously rescued them from cruel Egyptian slavery. From the blazing summit of Mount Sinai, He reminded them, " ' "You have seen what *I* did to the Egyptians, and how *I* bore you on eagles' wings and brought you to Myself" ' " (Exodus 19:4; emphasis added).

Like a mother eagle carrying her young, God had gathered His chosen people to Himself. Truly, the Lord loved Israel (see Deuteronomy 7:8).

With their best interest at heart, He proclaimed to them His law (Exodus 20). And they had responded with a firm commitment, saying, " 'All that the LORD has said we will do, and be obedient' " (Exodus 24:7). The freshly spilled blood of sacrificed animals ratified this commitment. "Moses took the blood, sprinkled it on the people, and said, 'This is the blood of the covenant which the LORD has made with you according to all these words' " (verse 8). That blood pointed forward to the sacrifice of Jesus Christ, who would someday die for their sins. An official relationship was thus established. The people of Israel had entered into a blood covenant with their eternal Lover and Deliverer. They were now His " ' "special treasure . . . above all people" ' " (Exodus 19:5).

Shortly thereafter, "Moses went into the midst of the cloud and went up into the mountain. And Moses was on the mountain forty days and forty nights" (Exodus 24:18). During those forty days and forty nights, God gave Moses instructions about the construction of a tabernacle, about its priesthood, and about the sacrificial system, which pointed forward to Israel's coming Messiah. That must have been an incredible time for Moses. Imagine camping out on the top of a mountain for over a month with your Maker! No other mortal has ever had such an experience. The climactic moment came when the Lord personally handed Moses "two tablets of Testimony, tablets of stone, written with the finger of God" (Exodus 31:18).

Amazingly, while these sacred events were occurring on top of Mount Sinai, there was trouble below. Because Moses had been absent for a long time, many Israelites became restless. They forgot about their blood covenant with God and returned to the superstitions they had practiced in Egypt. Incredibly, they even approached Aaron—whom Moses had left in charge of the camp while he was gone—and demanded, " 'Come, make us gods that shall go before us; for as for this Moses, the man who brought us up out of the land of Egypt, we do not know what has become of him' " (Exodus 32:1).

The golden calf

The result of this idolatrous movement was the casting of a golden calf. Then the shout rang out, " 'This is your god, O Israel, that brought you out of the land of Egypt!' " (Exodus 32:4). How tragic! How quickly Israel turned from her true Lover to a block of metal!

This very scene is the context of Exodus 34:5–7, which contains the proclamation of God's character. How would the Lord respond to this golden calf development? How would He relate to the guilty? Would He show mercy? What about His justice? Would He "visit" such bold iniquity? And if so, how? Negative natural consequences would surely result from bowing down to a statue of gold, but was that sufficient? Would the Lord just sadly pull back and withdraw His care, thus allowing Israel to reap what they were sowing?

The answer is No. Something more decisive was needed. "Such a crisis demanded a man of firmness, decision, and unflinching courage; one who held the honor of God above popular favor, personal safety, or life itself. But the present leader of Israel [Aaron] was not of this character" (PP 316). He wasn't fit for the task. He was too compromising.

The situation was critical, and something had to be done. Far away, near the top of the lonely mountain, the Governor of the universe began communicating special instructions to His servant Moses. A similar situation had occurred many years before, in the very shadow of His throne. Lucifer, the shining one, had not only denigrated God's character but also had influenced myriads of holy angels to shift their allegiance from the Creator to the creature. Simply permitting natural consequences to run their course wasn't enough. The stakes were too high. As always, there was a risk that God's reaction would be misunderstood; nevertheless, He knew what to do.

> And the LORD said to Moses, "Go, get down! For your people whom you brought out of the land of Egypt have corrupted themselves. They have turned aside quickly out of the way which I commanded them. They have made themselves a molded calf, and worshiped it and sacrificed to it, and said, 'This is your god, O Israel, that brought you out of the land of Egypt!' " And the LORD said to Moses, "I have seen this people, and indeed it is a stiff-necked people! Now therefore, let Me alone, that My wrath may burn hot against them and I may consume them. And I will make of you a great nation" (Exodus 32:7–10).

This is a most unusual passage. God told Moses not only to get down to the camp immediately, but also to let Him alone so that His *wrath* might burn against Israel and consume them. With unusual spiritual perception, Moses somehow discerned reason for hope and began interceding for his people, which is exactly what the Lord wanted him to do! Rejecting the apparent offer to make of him alone a great nation, Moses earnestly and unselfishly pleaded for Israel's salvation, and his plea prevailed. Whether or not you believe it, what followed was a perfect manifestation of God's love, mercy, and justice in the midst of a tough situation. And as we are about to discover, clearly, at least in this case, God's justice or "visiting" or "retribution" included much more than simply His allowing natural consequences to occur.

"Though God had granted the prayer of Moses in sparing Israel from destruction, their apostasy was to be *signally punished.* The lawlessness and insubordination into which Aaron had permitted them to fall, if not speedily crushed, would run riot in wickedness, and would involve the nation in irretrievable ruin. *By terrible severity the evil must be put away*" (PP 324; emphasis added).

Swift action was not only necessary but, according to the above quote, totally reasonable. Unless the rebellion was "speedily crushed," the entire nation would soon be involved in "irretrievable ruin." Such a disaster must not be allowed. The situation can be likened to a man with a deadly infection working its way up his arm and thus threatening his whole body. What should a loving and responsible physician do? Out of necessity, he might be forced to amputate the arm to save the man's life. Sometimes hard decisions must be made. If a doctor truly has his patient's best interest at heart, he will do what must be done. It was the same with God and Moses. It was time to act.

Moses' solemn act

Upon reaching the base of Mount Sinai, Moses was shocked to behold multitudes of Israelites dancing naked around a golden calf. Then his "anger became hot, and he cast the tablets out of his hands and broke them at the foot of the mountain" (Exodus 32:19). This solemn act testified to a corrupt people that because they had broken their covenant with God, He had broken His covenant with them.

The sound of the tablets shattering was heard throughout the camp. The party ended, and all eyes were suddenly riveted upon the face of Moses. Their leader had returned! As the Israelites beheld the intensity that his face expressed, many consciences were aroused. Thousands of revelers suddenly realized what they were previously blinded to—their great sin. "Then Moses stood in the entrance of the camp, and said, 'Whoever is on the LORD's side—come to me!' " (Exodus 32:26). *This was mercy's golden plea.*

It is vital that we realize that before the penalty for their sin was exacted, forgiveness was offered to each and every sinner, even to the worst offenders. "Those who had not joined in the apostasy were to take their position at the right of Moses; those who were guilty but repentant, at the left" (PP 324).

Silence momentarily fell—and was quickly followed by massive movement among the people. Husbands, wives, grandmas, grandpas, sons, and daughters either stood still or hurried in different directions, depending upon whether or not they had worshiped the golden calf. Exactly how long this regrouping took we don't know, but eventually three distinct groups materialized. People who hadn't bowed to the golden calf stood at Moses' right side, while those who had bowed but were responding to God's offer of mercy huddled nervously together on his left. When the dust settled, all eyes became fixed upon the middle group, which hadn't budged.

There they stood, bold, defiant, and unrepentant. "Hey Moses!" some may have shouted, "Who do you think you are anyway? What's wrong with a golden calf? The Egyptians worship cows. Don't be so narrow-minded!"

The awful moment had come. Standing at the base of a mountain whose summit was still enshrouded by a heavenly cloud, the middle group had refused to change. They had become a deadly threat to the eternal welfare of the entire camp.

At Moses' right hand stood the sons of Levi, who "had taken no part in the idolatrous worship" (PP 324; cf. Exodus 32:26). Throughout the degenerate debacle, this tribe had maintained unflinching loyalty to their blood covenant with their Lord and had firmly resisted the seductive influence of the middle group. With swift decisiveness, Moses "said to them, 'Thus says the LORD God of Israel: "Let every man put his sword on his side, and go in and out from entrance to entrance throughout the camp, and let every man kill his brother, every man his companion, and every man his neighbor" ' " (Exodus 32:27). The Levites obeyed this command instantly. They unsheathed shiny blades and began the terrible work of execution. When it was over, not a man in the center group remained standing. "So the sons of Levi did according to the word of Moses. And about three thousand men of the people fell that day" (verse 28). Israel had been purged.

We must analyze this event closely in our quest to understand God's character. First of all, Scripture reveals that Moses wasn't acting on his own initiative. Remember, he had just spent forty days and forty nights in the presence of his Maker. The Word also reports that Moses prefaced his death command to the Levites with the words "thus says the LORD God of Israel." Ellen White commented, "Those who performed this terrible work of judgment were acting by divine authority, executing the sentence of the King of heaven" (PP 324). Honestly, there's no way around it: the Lord Himself was behind this command. The Levites "were acting by divine authority."

It's also obvious that this visitation went far beyond "natural consequences." The middle group wasn't simply left alone to reap what they had sown. And in this situation, it is also quite clear that Satan and his angels didn't carry out the awful sentence. Whether or not we like it and or whether or not we understand it, the truth is that those in the middle group were directly executed by loyal Levites carrying out a specific command from God Himself. "Men are to beware how they, in their human blindness, judge and condemn their fellow men; but when God commands them to execute His sentence upon iniquity, He is to be obeyed" (PP 324).

The Levites' blessings

Even more significantly, the Lord specifically blessed the Levites for carrying out this difficult task. "Then Moses said [to them], 'Consecrate yourselves today to the LORD, that He may bestow on you a blessing this day, for every man has opposed his son and his brother'" (Exodus 32:29). This verse says that even relatives of the slayers were among the slain. A Levite may have executed "his son and his brother." Naturally, we cringe at this. Although we cannot now see the expressions on their faces, I'm sure those Levites cringed too. They weren't heartless individuals devoid of natural affection. Neither was Abraham when he was about to offer Isaac. No, none of these servants of God were inhumane or cruel. *Neither is the Lord.* The goal of this book is to make sense out of biblical stories—like this one—that we may consider inconsistent with God's love and mercy.

But back to the Levites. Significantly, the Lord put them in charge of His temple! "Those who performed this painful act, thus manifested their abhorrence of rebellion and idolatry, and consecrated themselves more fully to the service of the true God. The Lord honored their faithfulness by bestowing special distinction upon the tribe of Levi" (PP 324).

Notice carefully, those Levites performed an extremely "painful act." Not only that, but they were serving "the true God" as they did it. Yes, *the true God of the Bible commanded this fearful execution,* and it is our challenge to try and discern His reasons and to see His heart. To do this, we must lay aside our own opinions. Believe it or not, satisfying answers are available if we are willing to accept them.

"The Israelites had been guilty of treason, and that against a King who had loaded them with benefits and whose authority they had voluntarily pledged themselves to obey. That the divine government might be maintained justice must be visited upon the traitors. Yet even here God's mercy was displayed. While He maintained His law, He granted freedom of choice and opportunity for repentance to all. Only those were cut off who persisted in rebellion" (PP 324, 325).

Did you catch all of that? The golden calf story sheds light on such complex issues as "the divine government," "justice . . . visited," "God's mercy," and even "freedom of choice." It's all there. Those who teach the God-doesn't-kill doctrine maintain that because God values freedom so highly (which He does) and because He is so supremely good (which He is), He won't exercise any force at all, even to implement justice. But events at the golden calf disprove this theory.

People who promote the God-doesn't-kill doctrine often point to these lines: "The exercise of force is contrary to the principles of God's government; He desires only the service of love; and love cannot be commanded; it cannot be won by force or authority" (DA 22).

We believe this statement, but we feel it is being misused. Look closer. God's government will never resort to "the exercise of force" to produce "the service of love." It is "love" itself that "cannot be won by force or authority." God loves each of us, and He longs for us to love Him too, but He will never twist our arms or force us to obey—ever. The Lord prizes liberty. He grants freedom to all to either choose Him or reject Him. *But this doesn't mean that He will never use force to punish sin or put down rebellion.* Again, events surrounding the golden calf prove this. And this story is just one example; more are coming.

At the base of Mount Sinai, everyone had full freedom to make a choice. Not an iota of force was used to compel obedience. Even the worst offenders were offered pardon, which highlights God's mercy. But they had to respond to the gracious offer, and they didn't. When Moses pleaded "Come to me!" and the middle group adamantly refused, God could do nothing more for them. Then the Ruler of the divine government made a tough decision. He issued a command, loyal Levites sprang into action, and in a short time, three thousand perished who need not have died. Truly, their death was their own fault. It is in this sense that we understand the statement, "God destroys no man. Everyone who is destroyed will have destroyed himself" (COL 84).

The big picture

In order to really understand this bloody scene, we need to grasp the big picture. The following paragraphs explain exactly why an inherently loving, tender, and compassionate God did what He did. Read them carefully, "and may the Lord give you understanding in all things" (2 Timothy 2:7).

It was necessary that this sin should be punished, as a testimony to surrounding nations of God's displeasure against idolatry. By executing justice upon the guilty, Moses, as God's instrument, must leave on record a solemn and public protest against their crime. As the Israelites should hereafter condemn the idolatry of the neighboring tribes, their enemies would throw back upon them the charge that the people who claimed Jehovah as their God had made a calf and worshiped it in Horeb. Then though compelled to acknowledge the disgraceful truth, Israel could point to the terrible fate of the transgressors, as evidence that their sin had not been sanctioned or excused.

Love no less than justice demanded that for this sin judgment should be inflicted. God is the guardian as well as the sovereign of His people. He cuts off those who are determined upon rebellion, that they may not lead others to ruin. In sparing the life of Cain, God had demonstrated to the universe what would be the result of permitting sin to go unpunished. The influence exerted upon his descendants by his life and teaching led to the state of corruption that demanded the destruction of the whole world by a flood. The history of the antediluvians testifies that long life is not a blessing to the sinner; God's great forbearance did not repress their wickedness. The longer men lived, the more corrupt they became.

So with the apostasy at Sinai. Unless punishment had been speedily visited upon transgression, the same results would again have been seen. The earth would have become as corrupt as in the days of Noah. Had these transgressors been spared, evils would have followed, greater than resulted from sparing the life of Cain. *It was the mercy of God that thousands should suffer, to prevent the necessity of visiting judgments upon millions. In order to save the many, He must punish the few.* Furthermore, as the people had cast off their allegiance to God, they had forfeited the divine protection, and, deprived of their defense, the whole nation was exposed to the power of their enemies. Had not the evil been promptly put away, they would soon have fallen a prey to their numerous and powerful foes. It was necessary for the good of Israel, and also as a lesson to all succeeding generations, that crime should be promptly punished. And it was no less a mercy to the sinners themselves that they should be cut short in their evil course. Had their life been spared, the same spirit that led them to rebel against God would have been manifested in hatred and strife among themselves, and they would eventually have destroyed one another. *It was in love to the world, in love to Israel, and even to the transgressors, that crime was punished with swift and terrible severity* (PP 325, 326; emphasis added).

There you have it. Why did God do it? It was because of His love—love for the world, love for Israel, and even love for those in the middle group. Thus the execution of justice itself—the "visiting" part of His character—is rooted in the mysterious love of God. Take a close look at these quotes too.

God's love has been expressed in His justice no less than in His mercy. Justice is the foundation of His throne, and the fruit of His love (DA 762).

It is the glory of God to be merciful, full of forbearance, kindness, goodness, and truth. But the justice shown in punishing the sinner is as verily the glory of the Lord as is the manifestation of His mercy (LDE 240).

The nation of Israel had been divinely selected to become an earthly conduit so that salvation might reach the entire world. In Bethlehem, in the midst of that nation, a Baby would someday open tiny eyes. Thirty years later that majestic Man would walk on water, touch lepers, wipe away tears, and finally grip dark soil beneath olive trees the night before His death. The plan must be fulfilled. Nothing must stop it.

From the top of Mount Sinai, a heavenly Physician diagnosed a malignant tumor within the body of His beloved. Based on His eternal perspective, He knew what had to be done. A sharp knife was needed. And when the painful surgery was over, Moses, heavenly angels, and the tribe of Levi understood that *God did the right thing.*

Do we understand that?

For Further Thought and Discussion

1. Paul wrote, "Whatever a man sows, that he will also reap" (Galatians 6:7). Give some practical examples of how this sowing and reaping principle works in our physical bodies.

2. Does the sowing and reaping principle work in our relationship with God too? Explain.

3. Do you think that we can consider this principle to be a part of God's justice?

4. Does this principle contain any mercy?

5. How did God manifest His mercy after Israel committed the great sin of worshiping the golden calf?

6. How did He manifest His justice at the same time?

7. What does the golden calf incident teach us about God's justice?

8. Why do you think it is difficult for some people to accept the idea that God does sometimes actively punish sin?

9. How was the manifestation of God's justice in the golden calf incident also a revelation of His love?

10. What impressed you the most in this chapter, and why?

CHAPTER 4

A LOVER'S WRATH

The first duty of a man is the seeking after and the investigation of truth.
—Marcus Tullius Cicero

Many people have a difficult time reconciling God's love with His wrath, but as this book is determined to demonstrate, such apparently opposite extremes can be harmonized. In fact, harmonization is essential in our quest to comprehend the Lord's true character.

Before examining the wrath of God itself, it's important to realize how often the Bible mentions this quality. Here are just a few *wrath* passages in the Old Testament:

> While the meat was still between their teeth, before it was chewed, the wrath of the LORD was aroused against the people, and the LORD struck the people with a very great plague (Numbers 11:33).

> " ' "[God said], 'They have forsaken Me and burned incense to other gods, that they might provoke Me to anger with all the works of their hands. Therefore My wrath shall be aroused against this place and shall not be quenched' " ' " (2 Kings 22:17).

> The Lord is the true God;
> He is the living God and the everlasting King.
> At His wrath the earth will tremble,
> And the nations will not be able to abide His indignation (Jeremiah 10:10).

Neither their silver nor their gold
Shall be able to deliver them
In the day of the Lord's wrath;
But the whole land shall be devoured
By the fire of His jealousy,
For He will make speedy riddance
Of all those who dwell in the land (Zephaniah 1:18).

Now for the New Testament:

When he [John the Baptist] saw many of the Pharisees and Sadducees coming to his baptism, he said to them, "Brood of vipers! Who warned you to flee from the wrath to come?" (Matthew 3:7).

"He who believes in the Son has everlasting life; and he who does not believe the Son shall not see life, but the wrath of God abides on him" (John 3:36).

This you know, that no fornicator, unclean person, nor covetous man, who is an idolater, has any inheritance in the kingdom of Christ and God. Let no one deceive you with empty words, for because of these things the wrath of God comes upon the sons of disobedience (Ephesians 5:5, 6).

God did not appoint us to wrath, but to obtain salvation through our Lord Jesus Christ (1 Thessalonians 5:9).

This is just scratching the proverbial surface. A simple search in any concordance will reveal many other *wrath* verses. Obviously, this topic is terribly important and should be explored reverently, with humble hearts, for we are on holy ground when we're talking about the wrath of Almighty God! Surely we need the Holy Spirit's guidance, because "spiritual things" are "spiritually discerned" (1 Corinthians 2:13, 14).

There's no doubt that God's wrath is associated with His justice, which is a part of His character. In our last chapter we discovered that, while it is true that sin brings natural consequences, it is also true that at times God does act directly to punish evil. He did at the base of Mount Sinai when He inspired Moses to command the tribe of Levi to take up the sword. Remember, those "[Levites] who performed this terrible work of judgment were acting by divine authority, executing the sentence of the King of heaven" (PP 324).

So what about God's wrath? What exactly is it? Does it come from Him? Is it something God feels in His heart? And what about the increasingly popular idea that the biblical phrase *the wrath of God* merely means that the Lord decides to stop restraining the fury of nature, or the effects of sin upon sinners, or the machinations of the devil himself?

God hides His face

First of all, let us note that a careful study of the Bible reveals that there are many instances where God does indeed manifest His wrath *by withdrawing* from those who forsake Him and thus allowing evil consequences to occur. For instance,

> And the LORD said to Moses: "Behold, you will rest with your fathers; and this people will rise and play the harlot with the gods of the foreigners of the land, where they go to be among them, and they will forsake Me and break My covenant which I have made with them. Then *My anger* shall be aroused against them in that day, *and I will forsake them, and I will hide My face from them, and they shall be devoured.* And many evils and troubles shall befall them, so that they will say in that day, 'Have not these evils come upon us *because our God is not among us?'*" (Deuteronomy 31:16, 17; emphasis added).

Here God told Moses that after Moses' death many Israelites would "play the harlot," worship false gods, forsake Him, and break His covenant. "Then My anger shall be roused against them," the Lord predicted, "and I will forsake them, and I will hide My face from them." The net result of this divine departure would be that "many evils and troubles" would overtake the rebels. Yet all would not be lost. Verse 17 implies that God hoped the trials would awaken His people to return to Him. Thus, even in God's "anger," He remembered "mercy" (Habakkuk 3:2).

Still, Deuteronomy 31:16, 17 doesn't actually *define* God's wrath, as some suppose. It only demonstrates that the Lord often *expresses* His wrath by hiding His face and removing His protection. But does this prove that He *always* responds this way? We don't think so, especially when we look at the golden calf scene and at other biblical examples.

Some might counter, "So you believe that God is capricious and changeable, right?"

No, we don't. But when God said, " 'I do not change' " (Malachi 3:6), He was talking about His essential character, not about His methods. Our Creator is an infinite personality who has many options.

It seems to us that most everyone would agree that the Lord uses different methods to communicate truth. Paul wrote that God speaks in "various ways" (Hebrews 1:1). He has spoken through the Bible, through nature, through providence, through His prophets, through visions and dreams, by the Urim and Thummim, by the Holy Spirit directly, and above all, through His Son Jesus Christ. Does this mean that He changes? No, it doesn't.

Now notice carefully: concerning God's enemies, David wrote,

Then He shall speak to them in His wrath,
And distress them in His deep displeasure (Psalm 2:5).

By comparing Hebrews 1:1 with Psalm 2:5, we discover that God's speaking in "various ways" applies to His wrath too. So, He isn't tied down to only one method. (Notice also that Psalm 2:5 offers a good scriptural definition for God's wrath—it is "His deep displeasure." We will soon consider this further.)

Let's look now at another set of Bible texts—texts that concern the death of Saul, the first king of Israel. At first, Saul was humble, but by the end his reign he had drifted far from his Maker. As a Philistine army closed in for the kill, the disobedient king sought guidance from a sorceress who lived in a cave (see 1 Samuel 28). As a result of seeking her help, King Saul fully divorced himself from God's loving care, and shortly thereafter he died in battle.

Here's the issue: the Bible refers to Saul's death in two different ways. First, it says that when the Philistines surrounded him, "Saul took a sword and fell on it" (1 Samuel 31:4). In other words, Saul killed himself. But another text says that because he rejected God's word and "consulted a medium for guidance. . . . *Therefore He* [God] *killed him,* and turned the kingdom over to David the son of Jesse" (1 Chronicles 10:13, 14; emphasis added).

So which was it? Did King Saul kill himself, or did God kill him? Or are both somehow true?

Two different interpretations are now contending against each other. Those who believe the God of the Bible doesn't directly punish sin or take life often quote these verses about Saul as Exhibit A that proves their theory that whenever Scripture says God punished people, He really didn't but only "allowed" that "punishment" to happen. Today, many are calling this a new principle or a new paradigm that offers new light in contrast to the "traditional picture of God." They then apply this concept to every verse in the entire Bible from Genesis to Revelation that speaks of God's wrath, judgment, or punishment. They conclude that these verses about Saul comprise just one of the "proofs" that the Lord *never* really takes human life even though He says He does.

However, there are problems with this theory. First, while there are instances in the Bible where God apparently does "take responsibility for what He allows," we certainly can't apply this "God said it but didn't really do it" concept to *every* divine act in Scripture. For instance, the Bible says God created light. If we were to use the supposed Saul principle, we might ask if God really did create light or if the Bible just *says* He did. And what about "God sent forth His Son" (Galatians 4:4)? Did the Father really send Jesus, or did He only *allow* Jesus to enter our world? You get the point: we can't apply this supposedly "new paradigm" to every page in God's Word.

Second, there's another way to interpret what happened to Saul. Regarding a future invasion by Babylon, Moses told Israel, " 'The LORD will bring a nation against you from afar' " (Deuteronomy 28:49). Couldn't this also apply to the assault of the Philistines against rebellious King Saul? We believe so. And if this is the case, then when the Bible unapologetically states that the Lord "killed" Saul, this verse might not need to be so radically reinterpreted. It simply means that the Lord brought the Philistines against the doomed king. This comment fits perfectly: "*God will use His enemies as instruments* to punish those who have followed their own pernicious ways whereby the truth of God has been misrepresented, misjudged, and dishonored" (LDE 242; emphasis added).

Perilous interpretation

It is perilous to interpret some Bible passages in a way that requires a reinterpretation of all the rest of the Bible. Especially is this true concerning the proposed new paradigm, because it leads to the belief that God doesn't really mean what He says throughout the Scriptures. We must never forget that the very first Old Testament record of our adversary speaking (Genesis 3:1–3), and the very first New Testament one (Matthew 4:3) reveal him attempting to plant seeds of doubt about whether God really meant what He said. We should beware of this. In these last days when satanic trickery abounds, does it sound right to you that one of the keys for unlocking the true character of God is that God doesn't mean what He says? We don't think so, especially when we read statements like these:

> "Let us believe that God means just what He says" (HP 32).

> "We must believe that God means just what He says, and make no compromise with evil in any way" (RC 57).

> "Whatever contradicts God's Word, we may be sure proceeds from Satan" (PP 55).

We must take these solemn statements seriously as we deal with the character of God controversy.

Back to God's wrath. The primary section in the Bible that many now use to advance the theory that God's wrath is merely divine withdrawal is found in the book of Romans, chapter 1, verses 24–28. Paul sets the stage by stating, "The wrath of God is revealed from heaven against all ungodliness and unrighteousness of men" (verse 18). Then follows a dark catalog of human sins, such as pride (verse 22), idolatry (verse 23), sexual perversity (verses 26, 27), wickedness, deceit, murder, hatred, violence, and other evils (verses 29–31). Three times within these verses Paul declares that God "gave" people "up" or "over" to do these things: "God also gave them up to uncleanness" (verse 24). "God gave them up to vile passions" (verse 26). "God gave them over to a debased mind" (verse 28).

Some people have combined verse 18 and its reference to "the wrath of God" with the statements in verses 24, 26, and 28 that God gave various sinners up. Then they conclude that God's wrath literally means just that: "God gave them up," and that's it. By defining wrath in this rather passive, indirect way, they hope that they are portraying God as He truly is—a loving Being who isn't vindictive, harsh, arbitrary, or cruel. In their minds, if the Lord ever did act out of personal wrath, or if He ever personally punished evil, His goodness would be suspect. Then they go a step further by concluding that the entire notion of a sin-punishing God is a false doctrine that originates with the devil himself. Basically, they believe it's nothing more than a continuation of Lucifer's smear campaign that began beyond the stars. Those who teach this viewpoint know that we are in a war regarding who God is, and they adamantly contend that their "God isn't personally wrathful but just gives them up" interpretation of Romans 1 and other biblical passages lands them squarely on the Lord's side of this cosmic controversy.

But does it really?

Before we take a closer look at Romans 1 (and connect it with Romans 2), we wish to clarify a few things. First—and this should be obvious by now—we strongly agree that we are in a great controversy regarding who God is. Second, we also strongly agree that the Lord is *truly* good—in spite of Satan's false accusations against Him. Third, we fully believe that our merciful Maker isn't harsh, vindictive, arbitrary, or cruel—not in the least. Beyond this, we recognize that there are many times when God does withdraw His protecting care and allows either sin, natural elements, or evil angels to inflict suffering and pain. Yes, we agree with all of this. But here's a key divide: we adamantly *disagree* that divine wrath can be fully and adequately defined as "God gave them up," and we also firmly resist the conclusion that it is inherently improper, inappropriate, or even devilish for the Supreme Governor of the universe to actively, directly, and personally punish *real evil.* Here's why.

While Romans 1:24–31 does teach that God gives up sinners to wicked practices, nowhere in this chapter does Paul specifically define this giving up as the wrath of God. One of the practices Paul stated that God often gives people up to is sexual immorality (verse 26). The Lord did the same thing to those who lived in Sodom (see Genesis 19). Yet the Bible is clear that God's giving up of the Sodomites to sexual perversities occurred *before* His fire fell. In other words, *first* God gave them up to sexual wickedness, and *then* His judgment dropped from the sky. The Word reports,

"Sodom and Gomorrah, and the cities around them in a similar manner to these, *having* [first] *given themselves over to sexual immorality* and gone after strange flesh, are set forth as an example, *suffering the vengeance* [second] *of eternal fire*" (Jude 7; emphasis added).

The Bible states, "*The LORD* rained brimstone and fire on Sodom and Gomorrah, from the LORD out of the heavens" (Genesis 19:24; emphasis added). Did those burning flames really come "from the LORD out of the heavens" or not? If so, did God do a bad thing or a good thing? Genesis 19 tells us that on the night before that fiery destruction, almost the entire male population of Sodom surrounded the house of Lot, Abraham's nephew, and fiercely threatened to break down the door. Why? Because they wanted to abuse Lot's guests, who were really two angels in disguise. What a scene! In this case, if it really was the Lord who acted in fiery judgment, whom should we blame as unloving—God or the lusty Sodomites?

Paul's judgment warning

Back to Romans. After listing the degrading sins so prevalent among the Gentiles in Romans 1:29–31, Paul warns the Jews about not being too quick to judge, especially since they themselves were so prone to commit the same evil acts (see 2:1). Notice his convicting appeal: "Do you think this, O man, you who judge those practicing such things, and doing the same, that you will escape the judgment of God?" (Romans 2:3).

Look closely. The Jews were "doing the same" things those Gentiles were doing, which they had obviously already been given up to. Yet in this text, Paul makes two things clear: (1) "the judgment of God" is *not* synonymous with the giving up, and (2) this judgment is yet future. Not only that, but Paul also plainly warns that both groups—especially the latter— are fooling themselves if they think they will escape such a judgment. Paul continues, "Or do you despise the riches of His goodness, forbearance, and longsuffering, not knowing that the goodness of God leads you to repentance? But in accordance with your hardness and your impenitent heart you *are* treasuring up for yourself wrath in the day of wrath and revelation of the righteous judgment of God, who 'will render to each one according to his deeds' " (Romans 2:4–6).

Did you catch that? Paul clarifies that the sins that sinners are now being given up to are only increasing their accountability and are resulting in their treasuring up more "wrath [for] the day of wrath." Paul also identifies such wrath as the "righteous judgment of God." Significantly, at the end of verse 6, Paul adds that on the big day it will be the Lord Himself, not sin, other sinners, nature, or devils "who will render to each one according to his deeds."

In other words, in the long run, God isn't like a town sheriff who turns criminals over to even worse criminals for punishment. No, Paul wrote that it is God Himself who "will render" just punishments "to each one" based on individual deeds. If you think about it, this alone guarantees absolute fairness at the end. (More on this later.) This is the truth about Romans 1 and 2.

Jesus Christ warned, " 'As the days of Noah were, so also will the coming of the Son of Man be' " (Matthew 24:37). In Noah's day, "the LORD saw that the wickedness of man was great in the earth. . . . And the earth was filled with violence" (Genesis 6:5, 11). No doubt, God "gave up" the antediluvians to these evils things too. But once again, such giving up occurred *before* countless tons of water crashed down from the skies. However, this didn't happen right away. God was exceedingly patient. For 120 long years, Noah warned a doomed world about what was on the horizon. Few listened.

Genesis 6:6 offers a window into God's feelings: "The LORD was sorry that He had made man on the earth, and He was grieved in His heart." Our Creator is not an emotionless stoic in the sky, but One who feels deeply. His original plan was to create a peaceful planet populated by happy families and laughing children. But in Noah's day, He saw merciless cruelty, heartless violence, and crime, which brought great pain to His heart. He didn't want to see anyone drown beneath turbulent waves; nevertheless, He finally notified Noah, " '*I will destroy man* whom I have created from the face of the earth' " (verse 7; emphasis added). Again we ask, did God really do this, or did Lucifer send the Flood? Genesis 6:7 says God did it.

Now take a close look at the following quotation, which describes both the condition of that world and the subtle arguments put forth by those who rejected Noah's message: "As sin became general, it appeared less and less sinful, and they [the "wise men" of the earth] finally declared that the divine law was no longer in force; *that it was contrary to the character of God to punish transgression;* and they denied that His judgments were to be visited upon the earth" (PP 96; emphasis added).

Mark these words. The philosophers, scientists, and theologians of the pre-Flood world were quite confident that Noah was a deluded fanatic and that his message just couldn't be true. And according to the above statement, one of their primary "proofs" was the theory that it was "contrary to the character of God to punish transgression." Were they right or wrong? Obviously, they were wrong, and their error cost them dearly. May God help us to avoid repeating their mistake!

Yes, there are many examples in the Bible in which God manifests His wrath by withdrawing His protection and allowing the natural consequences to occur. But there are also many other instances in which He acted directly, which proves that it is *not* contrary to His character for Him to punish sin. In fact, the exact opposite is true—it actually *is* part of His character. Not only that, *it is a good part.* We already read about what happened at Mount Sinai and why God did what He did. An emergency had developed and the security of His people was at stake, so the Lord acted firmly and responsibly, motivated by love. A few other examples that can't be misinterpreted follow. We'll start with one from the Old Testament.

Nadab and Abihu

"Then Nadab and Abihu, the sons of Aaron, each took his censer and put fire in it, put incense on it, and offered profane fire before the LORD, which He had not commanded them. *So fire went out from the LORD and devoured them,* and they died before the LORD" (Leviticus 10:1, 2; emphasis added).

Nadab and Abihu were the sons of Aaron, the man who had made a terrible mistake by yielding to peer pressure and fashioning the golden calf. These two sons of Aaron, who had just been consecrated to the sacred office of the priesthood, partook of their father's lackadaisical spirit by failing to take their responsibilities seriously. After clouding their brains with alcohol, they marched right into God's tabernacle and offered profane fire contrary to God's specific instructions. The Lord had previously warned them about this (see Exodus 30:9), but they did it anyway. These men were brazen, foolish, and irreverent; and as leaders, their example was a disaster. "So fire went out from the LORD and devoured them, and they died before the LORD."

This fire flashed forth from *within* God's temple, and the Bible says that it was definitely "the LORD" who sent it, not the devil. To believe otherwise is to deny plain facts. Notice this straightforward comment: "Aaron's sons took the common fire which God did not accept, and they offered insult to the infinite God by presenting this strange fire before him. *God consumed them by fire for their positive disregard of his express directions*" (RH, March 25, 1875; emphasis added).

"God consumed them," the quote says. Yet here's something more serious; read on:

> Next to Moses and Aaron, Nadab and Abihu had stood highest in Israel. They had been especially honored by the Lord, having been permitted with the seventy elders to behold His glory in the mount. But their transgression was not therefore to be excused or lightly regarded. All this rendered their sin more grievous. Because men have received great light, because they have, like the princes of Israel, ascended to the mount, and been privileged to have communion with God, and to dwell in the light of His glory, let them not flatter themselves that they can afterward sin with impunity, that because they have been thus honored, *God will not be strict to punish their iniquity. This is a fatal deception* (PP 359, 360; emphasis added).

What a solemn statement! To imagine that "God will not be strict to punish" the blatant sins of those who have "received great light" is declared to be a "fatal deception." The first to flatter himself with such self-deception was Lucifer, who had the most light of all. He may have thought he could get away with it, but he was wrong. Such reasoning contributed to his determining his own fate. No doubt this "fatal deception" was also part of the weaponry he used to trick holy angels. Remember, Satan misrepresented God's character: "Thus he deceived angels" (DA 22). It's vital that we realize that misrepresenting God's character can swing both ways. People can misrepresent His love, kindness, and mercy or His justice. Both traps are equally dangerous.

Some think that direct judgments from God occurred only in Old Testament times, not in New Testament times; but this is incorrect. Let's look briefly at two direct New Testament visitations.

Ananias and Sapphira

The book of Acts tells the story of two members of the early church who tried to impress their fellow Christians with their generosity.

A certain man named Ananias, with Sapphira his wife, sold a possession. And he kept back part of the proceeds, his wife also being aware of it, and brought a certain part and laid it at the apostles' feet. But Peter said, "Ananias, why has Satan filled your heart to lie to the Holy Spirit and keep back part of the price of the land for yourself? While it remained, was it not your own? And after it was sold, was it not in your own control? Why have you conceived this thing in your heart? You have not lied to men but to God."

Then Ananias, hearing these words, fell down and breathed his last. So great fear came upon all those who heard these things. And the young men arose and wrapped him up, carried him out, and buried him.

Now it was about three hours later when his wife came in, not knowing what had happened. And Peter answered her, "Tell me whether you sold the land for so much?" She said, "Yes, for so much."

Then Peter said to her, "How is it that you have agreed together to test the Spirit of the Lord? Look, the feet of those who have buried your husband are at the door, and they will carry you out." Then immediately she fell down at his feet and breathed her last. And the young men came in and found her dead, and carrying her out, buried her by her husband. So great fear came upon all the church and upon all who heard these things (Acts 5:1–11).

This fearful event occurred among the followers of our Lord Jesus Christ, right within His church. Ananias and his wife, under deep conviction from the Holy Spirit, publicly declared that they would sell some property and contribute the entire proceeds to advance the gospel. Later, however, a spirit of selfishness surged, and they regretted their promise to give all the money to God. So, after they sold their property, they "kept back part of the proceeds" while blatantly trying to deceive Christ's Spirit-filled apostles by saying that their donation was the entire amount they received from the sale. Ananias lied to Peter and then fell down dead. Three hours later his wife walked in, also lied to Peter, and fell down dead too. The net result of this drama was that "great fear came upon all the church and upon all who heard these things" (Acts 5:11), and God's cause advanced. Notice these comments:

> God hates hypocrisy and falsehood. Ananias and Sapphira practiced fraud in their dealing with God; they lied to the Holy Spirit, *and their sin was visited with swift and terrible judgment.* . . .
>
> *Infinite Wisdom saw that this signal manifestation of the wrath of God* was necessary to guard the young church from becoming demoralized. Their numbers were rapidly increasing. The church would have been endangered if, in the rapid increase of converts, men and women had been added who, while professing to serve God, were worshiping mammon. This judgment testified that men cannot deceive God, that He detects the hidden sin of the heart, and that He will not be mocked. It was designed as a warning to the church, to lead them to avoid pretense and hypocrisy, and to beware of robbing God (AA 72, 73; emphasis added).

The death certificates of Ananias and Sapphira could not have correctly stated, "death by natural causes." Like Nadab and Abihu, they sinned in the very presence of God. They willingly lied, not to men only but also to the Lord Jesus Christ, whom they knew had recently laid down His life for their sins. Essentially, they were despising His love. But even more than this, the devil was seeking to use them to bring a spirit of covetousness—which is the exact opposite of the spirit of the gospel—into the heart of God's church. So, just as at the foot of Mount Sinai, "their sin was visited with swift and terrible judgment."

Significantly, the above commentary says that the judgment was a "signal manifestation of the wrath of God," which fell because of two things that God hates—"hypocrisy and falsehood." It was also "designed as a warning to the church." Lies are dangerous, even deadly. Remember what Exodus 34 says about God's character? He abounds in "goodness and *truth.*" The falsehood of Ananias and his wife was so flagrant and so contrary to God's truthful character, yet so secretive, that the Lord felt this judgment "was necessary to guard the young church from becoming demoralized."

King Herod

In the story as told in Acts 12, we see that King Herod was an evil, vain, cruel ruler. Inspired by dark forces, he "stretched out his hand to harass some from the church" (verse 1). He arrested Peter and threw him into prison, planning to execute him shortly. But then an angel of God appeared inside Peter's cell while the disciple slept. The Bible says that the angel "struck Peter on his side" (verse 7), woke him up, and led him to safety. When Herod found out, he mercilessly slew the innocent guards for letting their prisoner escape.

A few days later in Caesarea, with his hands stained in blood, Herod smugly sat on his kingly throne, wearing royal robes, and proceeded to give a speech. The crowd went wild, like a modern crowd at a rock 'n' roll concert. They screamed that it was the " 'voice of a god and not of a man!' " (verse 22). Herod was quite pleased with himself. He may even have imagined that he *was* a god—but at the very least, he did nothing to turn the crowd's worship from himself to the true God. His folly was short lived—his face contorted suddenly, and he collapsed in pain, for "an angel of the Lord struck him. . . . And he was eaten by worms and died" (verse 23).

Notice these insights from *The Acts of the Apostles:*

> The same angel who had come from the royal courts to rescue Peter, had been the messenger of wrath and judgment to Herod. The angel smote Peter to arouse him from slumber; it was with a different stroke that he smote the wicked king, laying low his pride and bringing upon him the punishment of the Almighty. Herod died in great agony of mind and body, *under the retributive judgment of God.*
>
> *This demonstration of divine justice* had a powerful influence upon the people. The tidings that the apostle of Christ had been miraculously delivered from prison and death, while his persecutor had been stricken down by the curse of God, were borne to all lands and became the means of leading many to a belief in Christ (AA 152; emphasis added).

The very same angel who rescued Peter became a "messenger of wrath" to Herod, who died in "great agony . . . under the retributive judgment of God." If Satan tempts you to ascribe cruelty to either God or His angel, resist his infernal whisperings. The real cruel one was Herod! He would have murdered Peter with fiendish glee. He executed his innocent guards and many others. What if one of those guards was your best friend or even your dad? Would you consider God "unjust" for sending His angel to strike Herod before he shed more blood? I doubt it.

Honestly, in every case referred to in this book so far—the Flood, the Sodomites, the golden calf, Nadab and Abihu, Ananias and Sapphira, and King Herod—God acted justly against willful, blatant sin. Radio talk show host Dr. Laura Schlessinger is famous for saying, "Do the right thing." Did Jesus do the right thing? We think so, and the Bible says so. Search your own heart. Even if we don't understand everything, we should trust Him and not blame Him. In time, we will understand fully. Then God's "character of love" will shine like the sun.

Here's one more verse that clearly disproves the theory that God's wrath must be entirely defined by Paul's phrase, "God gave them up." Read it carefully. "This you know, that no fornicator, unclean person, nor covetous man, who is an idolater, has any inheritance in the kingdom of Christ and God. Let no one deceive you with empty words, for because of these things the wrath of God comes upon the sons of disobedience" (Ephesians 5:5, 6).

These are the very same sins that Paul listed in Romans 1:24–31, which God "gave" people "up" to. Verse six plainly states "because of these things the wrath of God *comes*" (emphasis added). Notice that God's wrath upon these sins is *yet future*. We should "know" this, Paul stated in Ephesians 5:5. Then in verse 6 he warned, "Let no one deceive you with empty words." He was warning us to beware of deception about these very things.

Before concluding this chapter, let's look even more closely at the wrath of God. We must tread softly here. What you are about to read is simple, yet profound.

Notice again what Paul wrote in Romans 1: "The wrath of God is revealed from heaven against all ungodliness and unrighteousness of men" (Romans 1:18). God's wrath is "*against* all ungodliness and unrighteousness of men." In other words, it is *against* evil. When God contemplates wickedness itself, what do you think happens inside His heart? Is He entirely *nonemotional* about it, or does some degree of passion stir within the depths of His being?

The more one ponders this question, the more obvious the answer becomes. Sin ruined one-third of His angels. Shortly thereafter, it marred His perfect planet. Throughout human history since the Fall, it has been the real culprit behind every senseless murder, every painful divorce, every heroin addiction, every drunkard wallowing in his own vomit, every ruined life, and all the bitter tears of every devastated parent grieving over an abducted child. More than this, sin is also ultimately responsible for the agonizing cry of an only Son while nailed to a wooden cross, " 'My God, My God, why have You forsaken Me?' " (Matthew 27:46). So I ask you again, How do you think God feels about sin?

Here's a biblical answer. Paul wrote of the Lord, " 'You have *loved* righteousness and *hated* lawlessness' " (Hebrews 1:9; emphasis added). Take note that this verse mentions both love and hate. When we consider how much God loves us, don't you think that His love is connected to some feelings? Of course, it is. So what about His hate? Can God love and hate at the same time? Yes. In fact, when you truly love, you automatically hate the thing that hurts the one you love. Ask any husband who truly loves his wife, any wife who loves her husband, or any parent who loves his or her kids. It's perfectly natural to hate that which can destroy the one you love.

So what about God, the Supreme Lover? Isn't it logical to believe that if He truly loves, He will hate too? Yes, it is. And it's biblical. The true God of the Bible both loves and hates. And according to His Word, He does have personal wrath and even fierce indignation against evil. Just as there are two sides to every coin, even so God's intense wrath is simply the flip side of His unfathomable love.

Wrath defined

Notice this enlightening definition of the *wrath of God* found in *Nelson's New Illustrated Bible Dictionary:* "Wrath—the personal manifestation of God's holy, moral character in judgment against sin. Wrath is neither an impersonal process nor irrational and fitful like anger. It is in no way vindictive or malicious. It is holy indignation—God's anger directed against sin. God's wrath is an expression of His holy love."[1]

Perfect! *Nelson's New Illustrated Bible Dictionary* has it straight.

Yet don't miss this: God isn't the only One who hates. The devil hates too. But *what* God and the devil hate and the nature of their hatred differ vastly. The difference is greater than that between Republicans and Democrats. God and the devil differ even more than Martin Luther King Jr. (who promoted nonviolent reform) and the terrorist Osama bin Laden would. Satan hates the loyal angels and every human being. *He hates you.* And here's something else he hates: "The enemy of souls. . . . He hates everything which will give correct views of God" (4T 421).

The phrase *the wrath of the Lamb* appears only one time in the entire Bible, in Revelation 6:16. This verse applies to the end of the world. In context, it reads,

> Then the sky receded as a scroll when it is rolled up, and every mountain and island was moved out of its place. And the kings of the earth, the great men, the rich men, the commanders, the mighty men, every slave and every free man, hid themselves in the caves and in the rocks of the mountains, and said to the mountains and rocks, "Fall on us and hide us from the face of Him who sits on the throne and from the wrath of the Lamb! For the great day of His wrath has come, and who is able to stand?" (Revelation 6:14–17).

What is this "wrath of the Lamb"? The following paragraph reveals the answer. Read it carefully.

> Divine love has been stirred to its unfathomable depths for the sake of men, and angels marvel to behold in the recipients of so great love a mere surface gratitude. Angels marvel at man's shallow appreciation of the love of God. Heaven stands indignant at the neglect shown to the souls of men. Would we know how Christ regards it? How would a father and mother feel, did they know that their child, lost in the cold and the snow, had been passed by, and left to perish, by those who might have saved it? Would they not be terribly grieved, wildly indignant? Would they not denounce those murderers with wrath hot as their tears, intense as their love? The sufferings of every man are the sufferings

of God's child, and *those who reach out no helping hand to their perishing fellow beings provoke His righteous anger. This is the wrath of the Lamb* (DA 825; emphasis added).

There it is. How would *you* feel if you discovered that your precious child had been left to slowly freeze to death in icy snow by a group of uncaring, hard-hearted, "are we having fun yet?" pleasure lovers, who walked right past and did nothing? Wouldn't you be "terribly grieved" and "wildly indignant"? How would *you* feel as you beheld your child's empty eyes, staring vacantly into space while you clutched his or her lifeless, frozen form? Wouldn't you "denounce those murderers" with wrath as hot as your tears and as intense as your love? *This is the wrath of the Lamb, and it is far from passive!*

I still remember the night when our little son Seth, after quite a bit of encouragement from his parents, finally slept in his own "big boy" bed in his own room for an entire night. I slept on the floor nearby. Well, because he moved around a lot, he fell off his bed twice, banged his head on his bookshelf twice, and awoke sobbing twice! It broke my heart. Yet how would I have felt if an evil intruder had burst into his bedroom, seized one of his Thomas the Tank Engine toys, and tried to smash his head with it? Would I be able to relate to "the wrath of the Lamb"? More than you realize.

Ellen White, the little lady who lived in the 1800s, predicted that after thousands of years of incomprehensible patience toward gross evil and merciless cruelty, eventually, "justice will strike; for God's hatred of sin is intense and overwhelming" (RH, February 8, 1898). I'm glad this will happen. It encourages me to think that my God is such a Protector. It helps me to trust Him.

But what encourages me even more is the thought that, as much as God hates sin, He loves sinners even more. Whether or not you believe this, both the Father and His Son love you, and They want nothing more than to meet you and your family in heaven! They long to spend eternity with each of us. Let's not disappoint Them.

---

1. Ronald F. Youngblood, F. F. Bruce, and R. K. Harrison, eds., *Nelson's New Illustrated Bible Dictionary,* rev. ed. (Nashville: Thomas Nelson, 1995), s.v. "wrath."

For Further Thought and Discussion

1. Why do some people find it hard to accept the idea that a God of love can manifest wrath?
2. What are some popular misconceptions about God's wrath?
3. How would you define the wrath of God?
4. What are the differences between the wrath of God and the wrath of human beings?
5. Are there ever any similarities?
6. How is God's wrath ultimately rooted in His love?
7. How can people's upbringing affect their ability to correctly discern either God's mercy or His justice?
8. How can we overcome influences that may adversely affect our perception of God's character?
9. Some people define God's wrath as exclusively His giving up of sinners to the consequences of their sins. Can believing this theory negatively affect our relationship with the true God? If so, why?
10. What impressed you the most in this chapter, and why?

CHAPTER 5

WRITTEN WITH THE
FINGER OF GOD

Truth is beautiful, without doubt; but so are lies.
—Ralph Waldo Emerson

I still vividly remember scenes I saw on television dramas when I was a child—scenes in which some unfortunate man slowly sank into quicksand and was gone. Those memories remind me of the teaching of Jesus about the " 'wise man who built his house on the rock' " versus the " 'foolish man who built his house on the sand' " (Matthew 7:24, 26). The wise man, Christ essentially said, is someone who listens carefully to His words and puts them into practice, whereas the foolish man hears only casually and doesn't obey. When the storm hits, the wise man's house stands unmoved; but the foolish man's house comes crashing down, and great is its fall (see verse 27).

In the verse right before Christ's parable about the wise and foolish builders, He solemnly warned that on Judgment Day many unfortunate souls will hear Him say, " ' "I never knew you; depart from Me, you who practice lawlessness!" ' " (verse 23). These people won't be expecting to hear such frightful words, for they were quite religious (see verses 21, 22). If we look closely at Christ's statement, we discover that it establishes a definite relationship between knowing Him and the law. That's because, as we will soon discover, the law is simply a transcript of His character. Those who listen carefully to Christ's teaching, who humbly trust Him as their Savior, and who keep His law, are building upon the Rock, while those who don't will sink in quicksand.

Let's return to Exodus 34 and notice more details connected with the Lord's proclamation of His character.

And the LORD said to Moses, "Cut two tablets of stone like the first ones, and I will write on these tablets the words that were on the first tablets which you broke. So be ready in the morning, and come up in the morning to Mount Sinai, and present yourself to Me there on the top of the mountain. And no man shall come up with you, and let no man be seen throughout all the mountain; let neither flocks nor herds feed before that mountain."

So he cut two tablets of stone like the first ones. Then Moses rose early in the morning and went up Mount Sinai, as the LORD had commanded him; and he took in his hand the two tablets of stone.

Now the LORD descended in the cloud and stood with him there, and proclaimed the name of the LORD. And the LORD passed before him and proclaimed, "The LORD, the LORD God, merciful and gracious, longsuffering, and abounding in goodness and truth, keeping mercy for thousands, forgiving iniquity and transgression and sin, by no means clearing the guilty, visiting the iniquity of the fathers upon the children and the children's children to the third and the fourth generation."

So Moses made haste and bowed his head toward the earth, and worshiped (Exodus 34:1–8).

Immediately prior to Moses' trek up the mount, the Lord specifically told him to cut two tables of stone. Moses obeyed, and as he hiked, "he took in his hand the two tables of stone." When he arrived at Sinai's summit, the tables were in his hands. Then the Lord descended and proclaimed His character. The fact that Moses clutched the tables in his hands at the same time that God placed him in that " 'cleft of the rock' " (Exodus 33:22) should impress us deeply with the inseparable connection between what God wrote on those stone tablets and the proclamation of His character.

"I will *write*" (verse 1; emphasis added).

"The LORD . . . *proclaimed*" (verse 5; emphasis added).

First, God proclaimed His character, and then He wrote the details on solid rock. If you think about it, what God wrote *must* be a description of

His character, simply because He Himself did the writing. Would He write something contrary to His own principles? Of course not! This should be obvious, especially when we consider what God used to write with. It wasn't a pen, pencil, stylus, or writing tool. And He certainly didn't need Microsoft Word. Instead, He used His own almighty finger.

> And when He had made an end of speaking with him on Mount Sinai, He gave Moses two tablets of the Testimony, tablets of stone, *written with the finger of God* (Exodus 31:18; emphasis added).

> Now the tablets were the work of God, and the writing *was the writing of God* engraved on the tablets (Exodus 32:16; emphasis added).

> And *He wrote* on the tablets the words of the covenant, the Ten Commandments (Exodus 34:28; emphasis added).

Consequently, whenever men mock the Ten Commandments, they are really mocking God Himself, the Author of that law, even when they don't realize it. "In setting aside the law of God, men know not what they are doing. *God's law is the transcript of His character*" (COL 305; emphasis added). This is the awful situation of the doomed host who will finally hear Christ declare, " ' "I never knew you; depart from Me, you who practice lawlessness!" ' " (Matthew 7:23) This group foolishly pooh-poohed the Ten Commandments but never dreamed they were ridiculing the Writer of the law—Jesus Christ Himself. We must avoid this mistake. We have only one life to live; let's not blow it.

A careful comparison of what God verbally proclaimed to Moses in Exodus 34:5–7 (His character) with what He physically wrote on the tablets of stone (the Ten Commandments), reveals that God used the same words in both places. Note particularly the connection between God's character proclamation and the second and third commandments:

> And the LORD passed before him and proclaimed, "The LORD, the LORD God, merciful and gracious, longsuffering, and abounding in goodness and truth, *keeping mercy for thousands, forgiving*

iniquity and transgression and sin, by no means clearing the guilty, visiting the iniquity of the fathers upon the children and the children's children to the third and the fourth generation" (Exodus 34:6, 7; emphasis added).

"You shall not make for yourself a carved image—any likeness of anything that is in heaven above, or that is in the earth beneath, or that is in the water under the earth; you shall not bow down to them nor serve them. For I, the LORD your God, am a jealous God, *visiting the iniquity of the fathers upon the children to the third and fourth generations* of those who hate Me, but showing *mercy to thousands,* to those who love Me and keep My commandments" (Exodus 20:4–6; emphasis added [the second commandment]).

"You shall not take the name of the LORD your God in vain, *for the LORD will not hold him guiltless* who takes His name in vain" (Exodus 20:7; emphasis added [the third commandment]).

God described both His mercy and justice in Exodus 34:6, 7, and He did exactly the same thing in Exodus 20:4–7. He verbally proclaimed that mercy and justice are part of His character, and He wrote the same thing in His law. So, His law is a transcript or reflection of His character.

Both places also declare that God "visits." We must understand *how* He "visits," through allowing natural consequences and by direct action, and *why* He "visits," because of His intense love for people and His utter hatred of evil, in order to truly know Him *as He is.* Discerning this correctly will help us to be on the right side of the character of God controversy.

The definition of sin

Next point, the correct definition of sin. Exodus 34:6, 7 and the Ten Commandments both refer to sin. God told Moses He would be "visiting the iniquity" (Exodus 34:7), and the second commandment also speaks of Him "visiting the iniquity" (Exodus 20:5). What exactly is *iniquity* or *sin*?

Opinions and theories about what constitutes sin abound in the religious world, but our safety lies only in a plain "Thus saith the Lord." Man-made definitions are like quicksand, but what God wrote with His own finger is as solid as rock. When we humbly trust His words and fully believe what He says, we're on solid ground. Look again at the second commandment: " 'For I, the LORD your God, am a jealous God, *visiting the iniquity* of the fathers upon the children to the third and fourth generations of those who hate Me, but showing mercy to thousands, to those who *love Me and keep My commandments*' " (Exodus 20:5, 6; emphasis added).

Practicing "iniquity" is the exact opposite of loving God and keeping His commandments. That's what the second commandment states, and it was written with the finger of God. So, here the Lord has given us His definition of sin. It is breaking His law. Moses understood this clearly, which explains why, immediately after the Ten Commandments were first verbally proclaimed on Mount Sinai, "Moses said to the people, 'Do not fear; for God has come to test you, and that His fear may be before you, so that you may not sin' " (Exodus 20:20).

God has given you His law, Moses essentially said, *"so that you may not sin."* The evidence is inescapable. When we keep God's law by faith in Jesus Christ, we avoid sin. The entire Bible, including the New Testament, is rooted in this fundamental truth.

Paul wrote, "By the law is the knowledge of sin" (Romans 3:20).

James dittoed, "If you show partiality, you commit sin, and are convicted by the law as transgressors" (James 2:9).

John agreed, "Whosoever committeth sin transgresseth also the law: for sin is the transgression of the law" (1 John 3:4, KJV).

In these New Testament texts neither Paul, James, nor John was creating a new definition of sin. Instead, they were simply reiterating the truth God had taught in the second commandment. "Sin is," John wrote, "the transgression of the law." Will we accept God's definition or rely upon mere human opinion?

Some take issue with this definition by quoting Paul's words, "whatever is not from faith is sin" (Romans 14:23), which they interpret to be a superior, more enlightened definition of sin. But this can't be, for in the same book, Romans 3:20 and 7:7, Paul stuck to biblical facts by describing sin as the breaking of God's law. The solution to this apparent dilemma is not difficult. What Paul meant in Romans 14:23 is simply this: whatever doesn't come "from faith" leads to "sin," which is the breaking of God's law. We shouldn't pit Paul against Paul, or Paul against James, or Paul against John, and especially not Paul against "the finger of God." "Our only definition of sin is that given in the word of God; it is 'the transgression of the law;' it is the outworking of a principle at war with the great law of love which is the foundation of the divine government" (GC 493).

"God is love" (1 John 4:8), but His love is not a hodgepodge or mishmash of sentimental gobbledygook. To make it plain, God personally descended upon Mount Sinai and defined His love for all generations by inscribing, with His own finger, on solid rock His Ten Commandments. Paul understood this. That's why he wrote "love is the fulfillment of the law" (Romans 13:10). According to the Word, God's law is a transcript of His character; thus, disobeying His law is sin because it means disregarding both His goodness and His heart.

In the second commandment the Lord refers to those who "love Me, and keep My commandments." Herein lies a mighty truth. All true obedience (the "keep" part) must be rooted in love (the "love" part), and all genuine love for the Lord (the "Me" part) springs from an intelligent appreciation of His character, which includes both the mercy part and the justice part. "The law of love being the foundation of the government of God, the happiness of all created beings depend[s] upon their perfect accord with its great principles of righteousness. God desires from all His creatures the service of love—homage that springs from an intelligent appreciation of his character" (GC 493).

So far we have seen—from the Bible itself—that God is a God of love, that His character is a blend of mercy and justice, that His law is a transcript of His character, that our obedience to His law should be rooted in love and should spring from an intelligent appreciation of His character; and that breaking His law, which means going against His character, is sin. These are facts more solid than the United States federal government or the stability of Wells Fargo Bank.

More to the second commandment

However, there is much more to the second commandment. Upon

careful analysis, we discover that it goes far beyond simply prohibiting human beings from bowing down to statues of Dagon, Buddha, Krishna, or the virgin Mary. Take a look: " 'I, the LORD your God, am a jealous God, visiting the iniquity of the fathers upon the children to the third and fourth generations of *those who hate Me,* but showing mercy to thousands, to *those who love Me* and keep My commandments' " (Exodus 20:5, 6; emphasis added).

The second commandment not only defines iniquity, but it also reveals that there are two great classes of people on earth today. On the one hand, the Lord essentially informs us, are those who love Him and keep His law. On the opposite side are those who hate Him and break His commandments. We've already seen that while God always acts on principle, He has feelings too, and He hates sin with incomprehensible hatred because it is so malignant and destructive to those He loves. Yet the second commandment communicates the astonishing truth that some people actually hate God! Even more than this, it also tells us that hating God is often the hidden root of the "iniquity" that God visits.

This "those who hate Me" message is repeated many times in the Word. In the Old Testament, the prophet Jehu rebuked King Jehoshaphat for aligning with the wicked King Ahab, saying, " 'Should you help the wicked and love those who hate the LORD? Therefore the wrath of the LORD is upon you' " (2 Chronicles 19:2). In the New Testament, within his dark list of human sins, Paul includes "haters of God" (Romans 1:30). Jesus Christ also told His disciples, " 'The world cannot hate you, but it hates Me because I testify of it that its works are evil' " (John 7:7).

Thus, sadly, hatred of God often resides in human hearts. While such hatred may not be consciously recognized, all too often it's there. Ultimately, all such hostility originates with the dark angel who fell from heaven and whose original agenda was to usurp God's place—to dethrone the King of kings. In heaven, the devil would have killed Jesus if he could, just as Herod would have executed Peter. When Christ appeared as a man, Satan murdered Him (with God's permission). Once we grasp this, then we are prepared to understand the reality of what sin is. It's a hostile force in God's universe. It's an ugly manifestation of hatred of God and all He stands for. Lucifer hates Jesus with a personal hatred, and so he fuels sin. Thus sin is not merely a mechanical thing. Instead, at its hidden core, it's a personal affront, a direct attack, "the outworking of a principle at war with the great law of love which is the foundation of the divine government" (GC 493).

We're in a war, remember?

The big question is, how will the Ruler of the universe respond to such intense hostility? Will His response be entirely mechanistic, mild, and passive?

Far from it! Amazingly, His primary response, which has been flowing toward sinful humanity for thousands of years, has been one of love, not hate. Over and over again, God has shown compassion, not condemnation; kindness, not hostility; and mercy, not justice. Why? The main reason is simple: He truly loves His creatures no matter how mixed-up they are, and He wants what's best for them. The second reason is that from His infinite perspective, the Lord knows that much of the hatred people manifest against Him is rooted in their misunderstanding of His character. They don't perceive Him as He truly is, a God of love. Rather, they consider Him a tyrant—either because those who claim to know Him have grossly misrepresented Him or because they have been duped by the devil. Remember, Satan "deceived men. He led them to doubt the word of God, and to distrust His goodness. Because God is a God of justice and terrible majesty, Satan caused them to look upon Him as severe and unforgiving. Thus he drew men to join him in rebellion against God, and the night of woe settled down upon the world" (DA 22).

Tragically, what many hate is simply their own false perception of a god who doesn't actually exist. This is why " 'the only true God' " (John 17:3), the God of the Bible, waits patiently. Through His Holy Spirit, He constantly seeks to clarify to misguided souls what He is really like: "a God of justice and terrible majesty," yes, but also Someone filled with infinite compassion, incredible kindness, and a forgiving heart. (We will see this more clearly in the next chapter, where we zero in on the suffering of God's Son.) Even God's justice is rooted in genuine righteousness, and, of course, it is totally fair. However, there comes a time when mercy has exhausted all its resources and yet satanic hatred remains. Then finally— and it takes a long time for divine patience to reach this point—justice will strike. When it does, it will not only be truly just but filled with holy passion. The second commandment speaks the truth; read it yourself. His Royal Majesty declares, " 'For I, the LORD your God, am a jealous God, visiting the iniquity . . . upon . . . those who hate Me' " (Exodus 20:5).

This verse says that because people hate Him, the Lord will finally respond as a jealous God and visit their iniquity. The Hebrew word translated "jealous" is *qanna*. *Vine's Complete Expository Dictionary of Old and New Testament Words* says this word "refers directly to the attributes of God's justice and holiness, as He is the sole object of human worship and does not tolerate man's sin."[1]

Mirroring the language found in the second commandment, the following passage also describes God's personal and direct response to those who hate Him: " 'Therefore know that the LORD your God, He is God, the faithful God who keeps covenant and mercy for a thousand generations with those who love Him and keep His commandments; and He repays those who hate Him to their face, to destroy them. He will not be slack with him who hates Him; He will repay him to his face' " (Deuteronomy 7:9, 10).

This is strong language, but it communicates a key biblical message. God Himself will repay those who hate Him. *This is what the Bible says.*

A deep spiritual truth

It's time to state a deep spiritual truth before which we should take off our shoes, for it stands on holy ground. Here it is. To the extent that we fail to discern the seriousness, evil, horror, and malignity of sin, which is breaking God's law, which is the transcript of His character, *to that exact extent will we fail to discern the justice of God in punishing it.* Not only that, but we will then be in danger of perceiving the justice of God itself as evil. Even worse, we will think that God Himself is nothing more than a heartless killer.

Fallen human beings often misperceive God's justice and His character not because He really is devilish or a heavenly monster but because, like a man being arrested for drunk driving, they are "under the influence" of Lucifer's very first deception. Notice once again: Lucifer portrayed Christ as having "his [Lucifer's] own evil characteristics. . . . Thus he deceived angels. Thus he deceived men. . . . Thus he drew men to join him in rebellion against God, and the night of woe settled down upon the world" (DA 22).

Without the Holy Spirit's guidance, we can't see it. These issues are deep; may God help us to understand them.

It was Satan who first caused sinless angels to perceive the loving

Creator as evil. But really, what they saw was only Lucifer's dark heart superimposed upon God. What a trick! Thus he "deceived angels." Since his expulsion from Paradise, he has been working the same deception upon human beings. This is how he leads people to join him in rebellion against God. For thousands of years, our Creator has been merciful to all such uncalled for, misguided hostility; yet someday, in order to protect His loyal universe from adamant, incorrigible, and active wickedness, He will finally punish sin with holy fury, and *He will be perfectly just in doing so.* Even Lucifer will acknowledge God's righteousness on that big day.

But that day hasn't arrived yet (thus the need for this book). So far, because of God's ongoing patience (what earthly rulers would tolerate open rebellion against their governments?), sin hasn't been fully visited. Not yet. Nevertheless, something real does settle upon every transgressor of God's law. It's called *guilt.* What is guilt? *Merriam-Webster Online Dictionary* says it is "the fact of having committed a breach of conduct especially violating law and involving a penalty."[2]

It's true that human dictionaries don't always get things straight, especially when it comes to spiritual truths. Yet this definition is correct. Real guilt does come from "violating law," and it involves "a penalty." This is exactly what the second and third commandments teach. The second commandment defines sin as refusing to "love [God] and keep [His] commandments." This is the "violating law" part. And the third commandment refers to guilt. Our Creator declares, " 'You shall not take the name of the LORD your God in vain, for the LORD will not hold him guiltless who takes His name in vain' " (Exodus 20:7).

The Lord Himself will not hold anyone guiltless for taking His name in vain. In other words, He holds them guilty. The phrase, "not hold *him* guiltless" emphasizes personal accountability. *Him* is singular, which means that God holds people individually responsible—man by man, woman by woman, and young person by young person—for breaking His law. And this applies to all ten of the commandments, not just to number three.

Even more significantly, in the Bible, God's name refers primarily to His character. Exodus 34:5–7, one of the key passages in this book, also teaches this. While Moses hid in the cleft of a rock, God Almighty "proclaimed *the name* of the LORD" (verse 5; emphasis added), and then He revealed His character.

Put the pieces together. To take "the name of the LORD your God in vain" means more than common swearing, although it applies to this too. It also refers to the misrepresentation of God's heavenly attributes, whether by Jew or Gentile, black or white, Catholic or Protestant, clergy or layperson, Republican or Democrat, Adventist or evangelical. And since God's name is composed of blended attributes, this must apply to either misrepresenting His mercy or His justice. Either way, those who do so are not "guiltless." God Himself holds them accountable; that's what the third commandment says. And God proclaimed to Moses that He will " 'by no means [clear] the guilty' " (Exodus 34:7). In other words, the Lord Himself legitimately holds responsible those who are guilty, who break His law. "By no means" indicates that God definitely will not overlook their sins. There's no way around it. Excuses, self-justifications, and rationalizations won't work. The Hebrew word translated "clearing" is *naqah*. *The New Strong's Dictionary of Hebrew and Greek Words* says it means that the Lord will not "make clean," "hold innocent," or "leave unpunished"[3] those who break His commandments. And there is only one route to forgiveness (which we will focus on soon).

Tragically, this is a God whom many don't know. Multitudes today imagine that "the Man upstairs" is so nice that He will ignore human sin. Hidden in that cleft of a rock, Moses saw the truth. God is indeed kind and merciful, much more so than we realize, but He is also true and just, much more so than we realize. Sin is sin, and those who break any of His commandments and don't repent will not be acquitted, whether or not they realize it. Through the convicting power of the Holy Spirit, the law of God must be uncompromisingly presented to our mixed-up, twenty-first-century generation, so that sinners may discover their sin, their guilt, and their need for a Savior.

The first step in reconciliation to God is the conviction of sin. "Sin is the transgression of the law." "By the law is the knowledge of sin." 1 John 3:4; Romans 3:20. In order to see his guilt, the sinner must test his character by God's great standard of righteousness. It is a mirror which shows the perfection of a righteous character and enables him to discern the defects in his own.

The law reveals to man his sins, but it provides no remedy. While it promises life to the obedient, it declares that death is the portion of the transgressor. The gospel of Christ alone can free him from the condemnation or the defilement of sin (GC 467, 468).

The flip side of the truth about violating the law and God not clearing the guilty is the message of judgment. "Fear God," wrote Solomon, "and keep His commandments: for this is the whole duty of man. For God shall bring every work into judgment, with every secret thing, whether it be good, or whether it be evil" (Ecclesiastes 12:13, 14, KJV).

Some involved in the character of God controversy have expressed the opinion that in the judgment, it is primarily the Lord who is on trial, not us. While it is true that the universe is closely observing God's actions and that on the day of judgment He will be vindicated from all false accusations, it's far from reality to imply that human beings aren't being judged themselves. Those who advocate this "God is on trial not us" theory are usually quite hazy in their understanding of justice, law, sin, and guilt. But when we accept what Exodus 20 and 34 teach about these solemn realities, then the biblical facts about judgment fit right into place, just as easily as a correct key slips into a padlock. Then, with a click, the truth opens up. Notice what the Bible says about God judging man:

Rejoice, O young man, in your youth,
And let your heart cheer you in the days of your youth;
Walk in the ways of your heart,
And in the sight of your eyes;
But know that for all these
God will bring you into judgment (Ecclesiastes 11:9; emphasis added).

"The LORD will *judge His people*" (Hebrews 10:30; emphasis added).

"But I say to you that for every idle word men may speak, *they will give account of it* in the day of judgment. For by your words you will be justified, and by your words you will be condemned" (Matthew 12:36, 37; emphasis added).

This last passage—from Jesus Christ Himself—shows that people will "give account" in "the day of judgment" even for idle words. This must mean that hastily spoken words, though easily forgotten by the speaker, are recorded and will be exactly reproduced on Judgment Day. Not only are words recorded, but Solomon revealed that

> God will bring *every work* into judgment,
> Including *every secret thing*,
> Whether it is good or whether it is evil (Ecclesiastes 12:14; emphasis added).

Every man's work passes in review before God and is registered for faithfulness or unfaithfulness. Opposite each name in the books of heaven is entered with terrible exactness every wrong word, every selfish act, every unfulfilled duty, and every secret sin, with every artful dissembling. Heaven-sent warnings or reproofs neglected, wasted moments, unimproved opportunities, the influence exerted for good or for evil, with its far-reaching results, all are chronicled by the recording angel.

The law of God is the standard by which the characters and the lives of men will be tested in the judgment. Says the wise man: "Fear God, and keep his commandments: for this is the whole duty of man. For God shall bring every work into judgment." Ecclesiastes 12:13, 14. The apostle James admonishes his brethren: "So speak ye, and so do, as they that shall be judged by the law of liberty." James 2:12 (GC 482).

Make no mistake about it; in these quotes human beings are on trial, not God. It is the characters and the lives of *human beings* that will be tested in the judgment. Every act, word, and secret sin is recorded. Even the influence exerted for good or for evil is considered. If you think about it, it must be so. Adolf Hitler is dead, but his diabolical hatred of Jews—still showcased on Al Jazeera TV—often fuels further hatred on the Islamic streets throughout the Middle East. At the opposite extreme, Martin Luther King Jr.'s dead body may be rotting beneath his tombstone in Atlanta, Georgia, yet on the third Monday of every January throughout the United States, his nonviolent boldness still inspires millions of Americans—

both black and white—to love their neighbor as themselves. To this very day, Dr. King's famous "I have a dream" speech lives on. The same principle holds true of each dead person. Since Adam and Eve sinned, billions have died and been buried, yet " 'their works follow them' " (Revelation 14:13). This influence factor will weigh heavy in the judgment.

Does God kill?

Before closing this chapter we must address another issue dealing with God's law. We've looked at the third and fourth commandments, but in light of the character of God controversy, we would be remiss if we overlooked commandment number six, which states, "Thou shalt not kill" (Exodus 20:13, KJV). Because God's law is a transcript of His character, some have concluded that He Himself never takes life either, for if He did, He would be violating both His law and His character. What about this view?

We don't assume that the Hebrew word *ratsack,* which is translated "kill" in Exodus 20:13, does not mean "murder." The truth is that *ratsack* can be translated as either "kill" or "murder," which is why the King James Version of the Bible reads, "Thou shalt not kill," whereas the New King James Version reads, " 'You shall not murder.' " *The New Strong's Dictionary of Hebrew and Greek Words* includes both "murder" and "kill" in its definition of *ratsack,* along with "put to death" and "slay."[4] Thus, in our opinion, seeking to decipher the meaning of the Hebrew word for "kill" doesn't help.

But other facts do. That the statement "Thou shalt not kill" does *not* mean "Thou shalt never put anyone to death under any circumstances" is obvious from the fact that God Himself sometimes commanded the Israelites to put people to death—for instance, in the conquest of Canaan (see Deuteronomy 7:1, 2; Joshua 6:2–5, 21) and as a punishment in their judicial system (see Exodus 21:15–17; Deuteronomy 19:15–21). In both of these cases, God clearly told His people to take the life of other people. So, was He commanding His people to break His law? Or even worse, was He breaking it Himself? No, He wasn't. Thus the sixth commandment cannot mean "You shall never take life."

Of particular interest is what Romans 13 teaches about the relationship between God and civil government (verses 1–7). First, Paul says we should all be "subject to the governing authorities" (verse 1). Next he mentions the legitimate right of those authorities to administer justice within society. Now notice, "for he [the civil ruler] is *God's minister, an avenger to execute wrath on him who practices evil*" (verse 4; emphasis added). This is what those who serve in our judicial system do. They administer justice, "execute wrath," and sometimes take life.

Are correctional officials breaking the sixth commandment when they take a life in carrying out their duties? No, not if they perform their duties responsibly.

Now let's go a step further. If correctional officials can take human life without guilt and if they are "God's minister[s]," which means that they are God's representatives, then surely the Ruler of the universe, whom the officials represent, can do it too without violating either His law or His character.

Here's one more pertinent thought: when public servants "execute wrath on him who practices evil," this wrath is definitely not the same as passively giving "them up"!

At the beginning of this chapter, I mentioned those quicksand television scenes that remain etched upon my mind. As we near the chapter's end, another memory floats to the surface. The year was 1979, shortly after I became a Christian. One night I was sitting by myself in a hot Jacuzzi, nestled at the base of a dormitory at La Sierra College in Riverside, California, where I had just enrolled for my third year of college. Relaxing amidst aerating bubbles, I was reading Ellen White's *The Great Controversy Between Christ and Satan*. Upon reaching chapter 28, which is titled "Facing Life's Record," my eyes fell upon the following words:

> As the books of record are opened in the judgment, the lives of all who have believed on Jesus come in review before God. Beginning with those who first lived upon the earth, our Advocate presents the cases of each successive generation, and closes with the living. Every name is mentioned, every case closely investigated. Names are accepted, names rejected. When any have sins remaining upon the books of record, unrepented of and unforgiven, their names will be blotted out of the book of life, and the record of their good deeds will be erased from the book of God's remembrance. The Lord declared to Moses: "Whosoever hath sinned against Me, him will I blot out of My book." Exodus 32:33 (GC 483).

As I was sitting alone beneath sparkling stars, the Spirit of God moved deep within my soul. Conviction seized my conscience, and I sprang out of the comfort of those jets of warm water and knelt on the hard concrete surrounding the pool. My knees hurt, but I didn't care. *Oh,* I thought to myself, *I'm such a sinner!* It had been only a few weeks since God had rescued me from a life of marijuana smoking, cocaine snorting, disco dancing, and wild living. I had even sold drugs to my peers. Now I believed in Jesus, but the inner transformation had just begun. I was only starting to see things clearly. What about my past influence? What about the teenage buddies whom I had led astray? My mind went back scene by scene to various and sundry sins. Once again, but now with a deeper sense of my sinfulness, I confessed my ugly acts to God and relied on the blood of Jesus Christ. My only hope was Jesus, and I knew it.

The amazing thing about that experience was that, in the midst of an almost overwhelming sense of utter lostness and sinfulness, I felt a deep cleansing. Just as the stone was rolled away from the entrance of Christ's tomb, the heavy sense of guilt was being lifted off of me. One who will by no means clear the guilty was acquitting me because of my faith in the life, death, and resurrection of His Son. I sensed God's mercy, salvation, and, above all, His love. Oh yes, in His unfathomable love, He had paid *my* price! A nail-scarred hand was rescuing me from quicksand. He was setting my feet upon a Rock.

---

1. W. E. Vine, Merrill F. Unger, and William White Jr., *Vine's Complete Expository Dictionary of Old and New Testament Words* (Nashville: Thomas Nelson, 1996), s.v. "jealous."

2. *Merriam-Webster Online Dictionary*, s.v. "guilt," http://www.merriam-webster.com/dictionary/guilt (accessed June 12, 2008).

3. James Strong, *The New Strong's Dictionary of Hebrew and Greek Words* (Nashville: Thomas Nelson, 1997), s.v. "naqah."

4. Ibid., s.v. "ratsack."

For Further Thought and Discussion

1. Why did God write the Ten Commandments?
2. God wrote this law with His finger on solid rock (Exodus 31:18). What can we learn from this?
3. Why is it important to believe this biblical definition: "Sin is the transgression of the law" (1 John 3:4, KJV)?
4. What is so bad about sin? Why does God hate it so much?
5. The second commandment says that some people even "hate" the Lord. What are some of the reasons why they hate Him?
6. How can those who hate God be transformed into people who love and appreciate their Maker?
7. Why are *both* love and obedience important?
8. The third commandment states that God will not hold people guiltless who take His name in vain. What is the solution to such guilt?
9. Is there such a thing as false guilt? What might cause it, and what is the cure?
10. What impressed you the most in this chapter, and why?

CHAPTER 6

HEAVEN'S SWORD ON HEAVEN'S SHEPHERD

No sorrow can bear any comparison with the sorrow of Him upon whom the wrath of God fell with overwhelming force.

—Ellen G. White, AG 168.

"When the fullness of the time had come, God sent forth His Son" (Galatians 4:4). My wife, Kristin, and I have two children, which makes us appreciate this verse as never before. At the time of this writing, our son, Seth, is nearly three and a half years old and little Abigail Rose arrived just two weeks ago. Dr. Lewis and Lela have a five-and-a-half-year-old girl, Hadassah, and Lela is now expecting another child. Being a parent is absolutely fantastic. We wouldn't trade it for anything.

Most of us, as parents, feel that our children are part of us. In a very real sense, what happens to them happens to us. When they're happy, we're happy. When they suffer, we suffer too. Words can never fully explain this intimate parent-child connection because its roots originate beyond the stars, in a heavenly Godhead comprised of the Father, the Son, and the Holy Spirit. How close are They? No one really knows, for Their relationship is eternal. Even sinless angels can't fully comprehend it.

What then can be said about these five words: "God sent forth His Son" (Galatians 4:4)? Obviously, the Father didn't have to send His Son, and Jesus didn't have to go. But They both chose this route willingly for one primary reason: Their intense mutual love for lost humanity. " 'For God *so loved* the world,' " states the most famous verse in the Bible, " 'that He gave His only begotten Son, that whoever believes in Him should not perish but have everlasting life' " (John 3:16; emphasis added). God has only one eternal Son, yet He was willing to see Him mocked, beaten, spat upon, and even crucified on a shaft of wood to save us from sin. I can't imagine watching that happen to my little boy. Tears form in my eyes at the mere thought!

But what of God? When He sent His Son into the world,

> Sin had become a science, and vice was consecrated as a part of religion. Rebellion had struck its roots deep into the heart, and the hostility of man was most violent against heaven. . . .
>
> With intense interest the unfallen worlds had watched to see Jehovah arise, and sweep away the inhabitants of the earth. And if God should do this, Satan was ready to carry out his plan for securing to himself the allegiance of heavenly beings. He had declared that the principles of God's government make forgiveness impossible. Had the world been destroyed, he would have claimed that his accusations were proved true. He was ready to cast blame upon God, and to spread his rebellion to the worlds above. *But instead of destroying the world, God sent His Son to save it.* . . . Through every age, through every hour, the love of God had been exercised toward the fallen race. Notwithstanding the perversity of men, the signals of mercy had been continually exhibited. And when the fullness of the time had come, the Deity was glorified by pouring upon the world a flood of healing grace that was never to be obstructed or withdrawn till the plan of salvation should be fulfilled (DA 37; emphasis added).

How marvelous! Unnumbered books have been written about the unfathomable descent of our Lord Jesus Christ from His heavenly home into Mary's body, to the manger, to the streets of Nazareth, to the land of Israel. We can learn countless lessons as we contemplate His earthly pilgrimage. Yet the focus of this book is the character of God controversy. With this in mind, it's time that we enter the darkness of Gethsemane and the clouds of Calvary.

The Shepherd struck

On that fateful Thursday evening nearly two thousand years ago, Jesus and His disciples had just finished eating the Passover meal. As they walked together, "Jesus said to them, 'All of you will be made to stumble because of Me this night, for it is written:

"I will strike the Shepherd,
And the sheep of the flock will be scattered" ' " (Matthew 26:31).

In the twenty-eight years that I have been a Christian, I have never heard even one sermon that has quoted or sought to explain this text; yet it is filled with power, mystery, and hidden depth. Jesus told His disciples what was about to happen to Him on that very night because it was written in the Old Testament. "I will strike the Shepherd," He quoted, "And the sheep of the flock will be scattered." This cryptic text comes from Zechariah 13:7. The entire verse reads,

"Awake, O sword, against My Shepherd,
Against the Man who is My Companion,"
Says the LORD of hosts.
"Strike the Shepherd,
And the sheep will be scattered;
Then I will turn My hand against the little ones."

Jesus was approaching Gethsemane when He quoted this verse. Within a few minutes, even before He reached the Garden, something began happening to Him that differed from anything He had ever experienced before. For three and a half years, He had battled hard-hearted humans and desperate demons. It hadn't been easy. Yet those struggles were only horizontal, not vertical—in every conflict, God's peace had remained in His heart. But now, for the first time ever, the unity that had existed between Jesus and His Father was disintegrating. The strain Jesus bore was excruciating. "As [the disciples] approached the garden, [they] had marked the change that came over their Master. Never before had they seen Him so utterly sad and silent. . . . His form swayed as if He were about to fall. . . . Every step that He now took was with labored effort. He groaned aloud, as if suffering under the pressure of a terrible burden. Twice His companions supported Him, or He would have fallen to the earth" (DA 685, 686).

After what must have seemed like hours, Jesus and His little band reached the olive trees. As Jesus' strength ebbed away, He told eight of His disciples to tarry near the gate, while He took Peter, James, and John into the Garden's inner recesses. "And He began to be sorrowful and

deeply distressed. Then He said to them, 'My soul is exceedingly sorrowful, even to death' " (Matthew 26:37, 38).

These verses reveal that Jesus was beginning to feel something un-
imaginably painful. The experience was unique and overwhelmingly
dark. It penetrated far beyond the body. "My soul," Jesus moaned, "is
exceedingly sorrowful, even to death." It's important to realize that the
source of this fierce conflict was invisible. No human hand had yet been
laid on Him, no spit had wet His face, no temple guards had physically
abused Him, nor had Jesus yet felt any whip or nails. And Satan certainly wasn't inside of Him. No. The pressure of that "terrible burden"
had to do with sin and with His Father.

What was going on? Here's the answer: "Upon Him who knew no sin
must be laid the iniquity of us all. So dreadful does sin appear to Him, so
great is the weight of guilt which He must bear, that He is tempted to fear
it will shut Him out forever from His Father's love. *Feeling how terrible is
the wrath of God against transgression,* He exclaims, 'My soul is exceeding
sorrowful, even unto death' " (DA 685; emphasis added).

This paragraph is amazing. It mentions both "His Father's love" and
"the wrath of God against transgression." Both are real, and we shouldn't
overemphasize one to the exclusion of the other. If you find this is hard to
understand, welcome to the club. Even holy angels seek to comprehend
this mystery. All His life Jesus had walked in the light of His Father's love,
and that love had not changed. But something had. The terrible weight of
human guilt was upon Him. Eternal justice was closing in.

> Christ was now standing in a different attitude from that in
> which He had ever stood before. His suffering can best be described
> in the words of the prophet, "Awake, O sword, against My shep-
> herd, and against the man that is My fellow, saith the Lord of hosts."
> [Zechariah] 13:7. As the substitute and surety for sinful man, *Christ
> was suffering under divine justice. He saw what justice meant.* Hith-
> erto He had been as an intercessor for others; now He longed to
> have an intercessor for Himself (DA 686; emphasis added).

The paragraph above lies at the heart of this book. Christ's suffering,
we are told, "can *best* be described" by what is written in Zechariah
13:7, "Awake, O sword, against my shepherd, and against the man that

is my fellow" (KJV). The language is both graphic and active. A sword had been unsheathed, and its cold, steely blade was now piercing God's "fellow"—His own Son. Believe it or not, this blade was the sword of justice, which had slumbered ever since Adam and Eve ate the forbidden fruit.

Seeing what justice meant

Up to this point, human history had been speckled with tiny pricks from this sword, but never before had it struck like this. For thousands of years, mercy largely prevailed. And even on those rare occasions when God's judgments did fall, they affected only the body, never the soul. But this was different. What was happening in Gethsemane was unique. "Christ was suffering under divine justice. He saw what justice meant."

For the first time ever, the sword of justice had reached the level of the soul. *His soul.*

> The sins of men weighed heavily upon Christ, and the sense of God's wrath against sin was crushing out His life (DA 687).

> The sword of justice was unsheathed, and the wrath of God against iniquity rested upon man's substitute, Jesus Christ, the only begotten of the Father (AG 168).

> Voluntarily our divine Substitute bared His soul to the sword of justice, that we might not perish but have everlasting life (1 SM 322).

The Hebrew word translated "sword" in Zechariah 13:7 is *chereb. The New Strong's Dictionary of Hebrew and Greek Words* defines *chereb* as "a *cutting* instrument (from its *destructive* effect), as a *knife, sword,* or other sharp implement."[1] As for the word *justice, Merriam-Webster Online Dictionary* includes these definitions: "the maintenance or administration of what is just," "the administration of law," "the quality of being just, impartial, or fair."[2] In other words, the "sword of justice" is the strict, impartial, knifelike administration of what is just, right, and fair. The sword of this justice began to fall upon God's dear Son in Gethsemane.

Why? Wasn't Jesus entirely pure and guiltless?

Yes. But "the sins of men weighed heavily upon Christ." Mysteriously, in a way we can't fully comprehend, the sum total of humanity's accumulated sin and guilt—all the sins committed from the time of Adam to the end—was being transferred to Him. So, at that time, as never before, the justice part of the divine government was dealing fully with all that sin.

Satan desperately wants to cloud our minds about what was really happening. When we hear about this sword of justice, he works furiously to distort facts and blind us to the truth. He says to us, "What a harsh, cruel, and arbitrary God you serve! Anybody who would murder his own son must be a monster. How can you trust such a tyrant?"

Don't be deceived by Satan's twisted reasoning. Remember, the devil seeks to misrepresent the Lord's character. " 'He is a liar and the father of it' " (John 8:44).

The unsheathing of this sword was real, not imaginary. Yet it is vital to comprehend that in all of this, God was not being bad, but good. He wasn't being unfair, but fair. He wasn't being overly strict or cruel, but perfectly balanced and righteous. And the fact that both Jesus Christ and His Father were cooperating together in this amazing venture reveals something even more incomprehensible—something that gives an entirely new depth to a common word. That word is *mercy*. Believe it or not, the heavenly hand that gripped that sword did so in mercy. And behind that hand beat a loving heart—*a heart willing to sacrifice everything to save our souls!*

Why then such severe, intense language? Why not use a milder expression, something more congenial and palatable? The language of Zechariah 13:7 warns us to "awake." The Lord wants to awaken us to the horror of sin. He wants Satan's anesthetic to wear off. Then we will taste the filth, feel the conviction, and sense the nightmare of what sin really is. *Sin, not God, is the enemy!*

> Behold [Jesus] contemplating the price to be paid for the human soul. In His agony He clings to the cold ground, as if to prevent Himself from being drawn farther from God. The chilling dew of night falls upon His prostrate form, but He heeds it not. From His pale lips comes the bitter cry, "O My Father, if it

be possible, let this cup pass from Me." Yet even now He adds, "Nevertheless not as I will, but as Thou wilt" (DA 687).

At the beginning of this chapter I wrote about the love parents have for their children. Gethsemane's dark night reveals the struggle of a Father and His Son. Words fail me. As Jesus "clings to the cold ground," They are being separated from each Other. Couldn't They have avoided this? Couldn't the Lord just overlook sin, bypass human guilt, and simply wrap His loving arms around sinners who choose to come home?

Some, in their teaching, almost imply that He could have done this. Based on their stated views, it seems that the only thing that needs to be dealt with is our false view of God's love. Once we see how good He is and begin to trust Him, the entire problem is solved—we're in, saved. But this perspective leaves too much unsaid. Yes, we need to see God's love. Yes, it is "the goodness of God" that leads us to repentance (Romans 2:4). But God's "goodness" goes far beyond mere niceness. We can't ignore His justice. *He had to deal with sin.* The sword was unavoidable.

"There was silence in heaven. No harp was touched. Could mortals have viewed the amazement of the angelic host as in silent grief they watched the Father separating His beams of light, love, and glory from His beloved Son, they would better understand how offensive in His sight is sin" (DA 693).

The sentences above raise a core issue: how offensive God regards sin to be. As I stated before, to the degree that we recognize how ugly sin really is, to that same degree will we uphold, support, and even appreciate God's justice against it. Conversely, to the extent that we fail to discern sin's maliciousness, to that same extent will we mistakenly attribute harshness, injustice, or even cruelty to the Lord for condemning it.

To those who fall into the latter camp, God's retributions seem offensive, whether they were directed against Cain, the antediluvians, the men of Sodom, Nadab and Abihu, the golden calf idolaters, Ananias and Sapphira, or King Herod. Those who yield to Satan's subtle stratagem of investing our loving Creator with Satan's own evil characteristics will perceive the Lord as a bad guy—an unreasonable meany in the sky. But this is a complete delusion. When we ponder what happened in Gethsemane, we are enabled to understand the issues better. Then the lights go on and we see clearly. Then we ask, "Is sin so bad that it separated the

Father from His Son?" We are jolted into reality. And then we can understand the sword.

"Let this cup pass"

" 'O My Father,' " Jesus moaned, " 'if it is possible, let this cup pass from Me' " (Matthew 26:39). What did He mean by "this cup"? Obviously, He wasn't holding a literal container in His hands. The key that unlocks this mystery is found in the book of Revelation. After the close of human probation (more on this later), those who receive the mark of the beast will "drink of the wine of *the wrath of God,* which is poured out without mixture into *the cup* of his indignation" (Revelation 14:10, KJV; emphasis added). So, Revelation 14 describes an apocalyptic "cup" inside of which is "the wine of the wrath of God."

Revelation 14:10 says that wine is poured out "without mixture." The Greek word translated "without mixture" is *akratos. Vine's Complete Expository Dictionary of Old and New Testament Words* says *akratos* means "unrestrained."[3] *The New Strong's Dictionary of Hebrew and Greek Words* adds "undiluted"[4] in its definition. And the enhanced Strong's lexicon says "unmixed, pure."[5] Thus "the wine of the wrath of God" frothing inside that apocalyptic cup is "unrestrained," "undiluted," "pure," and "unmixed." The key question is unmixed with what? The answer is *unmixed with mercy.* In other words, the wrath described in Revelation 14:10 has not one drop of mercy mixed into it. Notice the following quotes describing that fearful time when such wrath is finally "poured out."

> Men are prone to abuse the long-suffering of God, and to presume on His forbearance. But there is a point in human iniquity when it is time for God to interfere; and terrible are the issues. "The Lord is slow to anger, and great in power, and will not at all acquit the wicked" (Nahum 1:3). The long-suffering of God is wonderful, because He puts constraint on His own attributes; but punishment is nonetheless certain. Every century of profligacy has treasured up wrath against the day of wrath; and when the time comes, and the iniquity is full, then God will do His strange work. It will be found a terrible thing to have worn out the divine patience; *for the wrath of God will fall so signally and strongly that it is*

presented as being unmixed with mercy; and the very earth will be desolated (2 SM 372, 373; emphasis added).

All the judgments upon men, prior to the close of probation, have been mingled with mercy. The pleading blood of Christ has shielded the sinner from receiving the full measure of his guilt; but in the final judgment, *wrath is poured out unmixed with mercy* (GC 629; emphasis added).

It was the decision to drink the wine conveyed in this cup that Jesus struggled with in Gethsemane. " 'O My Father,' " He groaned aloud, " 'if this cup cannot pass away from Me unless I drink it, Your will be done' " (Matthew 26:42). Throughout history, no one else has swallowed such a brew—ever. Jesus realized what it involved. "He saw what justice meant" (DA 686). He knew it meant separation from His Father, and it meant bearing the full weight of God's wrath against sin, without mercy! At this point, Jesus was "overcome by the horror of a great darkness" (DA 690). His mental agony was so intense that "His sweat became like great drops of blood falling down to the ground" (Luke 22:44). If an angel hadn't come to strengthen Him, He would have expired among the olive trees. He never would have made it to Calvary.

I once heard about a father who told his little boy to climb a ladder. "Jump into my arms," he told his son. "I'll catch you." Trusting his dad implicitly, the boy confidently jumped. But then the father unexpectedly stepped aside, and the child's face smacked the ground. "Let that be a lesson to you," the dad declared coldly. "Never trust anyone." How awful! I'm thankful that our Father in heaven would never let His children hit the ground like that—that is, if He could possibly prevent it. With arms as strong as eternity, He would hold them fast.

However, in Gethsemane, the Father longed to protect Jesus, but He couldn't. The conflict was terrible. God's own attributes clashed within His immortal heart. Love, mercy, and justice tossed, turned, and churned in ways that mortals will never completely comprehend. Holy angels gazed on the scene in silence. Demons trembled. Would Jesus go through with it—*the wrath of God unmixed with mercy*? Three times He prayed for release. " 'O My Father' "! He whispered the third and final time. " 'If this cup cannot pass away from Me unless I drink it, Your will be done.' "

"Having made the decision, [Jesus] fell dying to the ground" (DA 693). "He had borne that which no human being could ever bear; for He had tasted the sufferings of death for every man" (ibid., 694).

Now let's fast-forward approximately eight hours—past Judas's betrayal, Peter's denial, two trials before the Sanhedrin, one trial before Herod, two more before Pilate, thirty-nine lashes, a piercing crown of thorns, and three Roman spikes—to that fearful time when the Son of God hung between two thieves. The blood of millions of lambs, sheep, doves, goats, and bulls foreshadowed this time. The godly line of Seth, patriarchs and prophets, and the faithful of Israel throughout all ages had anxiously awaited it. Heaven's clock now struck the hour. This was it. As we contemplate Calvary, our focus here is the character of God controversy. What does the Cross reveal about our Maker? What really happened that Friday afternoon outside Jerusalem?

What really happened?

First, we must understand that Jesus' suffering far exceeded the physical pain caused by nails and thorns. The Bible emphatically declares, "Christ died for our sins according to the Scriptures" (1 Corinthians 15:3). Thus His primary agony was spiritual. Scripture defines sin as "the transgression of the law" (1 John 3:4, KJV). Thus the deeper pain Jesus felt was the pain of experiencing *our breaking of God's law,* which had been mysteriously laid upon His sinless soul. Therefore when anyone—whether priest, rabbi, pastor, layperson, professor, scholar, or Bible teacher—speaks disparagingly of the Ten Commandments, they know not what they do. Without realizing it, they are attacking Jesus Himself, His character, and His plan of salvation. "No heart that is stirred with enmity against the law of God is in harmony with Christ, who suffered on Calvary to vindicate and exalt the law before the universe" (FW 95).

Next, the intensity of Jesus Christ's suffering in the Garden of Gethsemane and on Calvary reveals to our astonished vision as nothing else can, the true horror of sin and the reality of God's hostility against it. Sin is so bad, and the Lord hates it so much, that He spared not His own precious Son to get rid of it! The spell Lucifer has cast upon our minds must be broken so that we can discern this truth. Sin is more evil than we realize. It is a mortal threat to the eternal well-being of humans, angels, and the universe. God despises it as the greatest offender. "*The offensive character of sin can be estimated only in the light of the cross.* When men urge that God is too merciful to punish the transgressors of his law, let them look to Calvary; let them realize that it was because Christ took upon himself the guilt of the disobedient, and suffered in the sinner's stead, *that the sword of justice was awakened against the Son of God*" (ST, January 6, 1881; emphasis added).

Some teach that rather than a divine atonement for sin itself, Jesus Christ's sacrifice is merely a demonstration that sin results in death. They believe that when God told Adam and Eve that if they sinned they would surely die (see Genesis 2:17), He told the truth, and that He then merely demonstrated His truthfulness by allowing His Son to die on Calvary. But this is a half-truth. Yes, sin leads to death; and yes, God told the truth. But the cross is much more than a mere demonstration.

The apostle John wrote that Jesus "is the propitiation for our sins, and not for ours only but also for the whole world" (1 John 2:2). Thus Jesus died for the sins of the whole world. All of our violations of God's law—yours, mine, everyone's—were literally and mysteriously placed upon Him. "The LORD [the Father] has laid on Him [the Son] the iniquity of us all" (Isaiah 53:6). Jesus Christ died *in our place,* as our *Substitute,* because we broke His law. The sanctuary service taught this every time an innocent animal had its throat slit. The animal died *instead* of the sinner.

As the *substitute* and surety for sinful man, Christ was suffering under divine justice. He saw what justice meant (DA 686; emphasis added).

[Jesus] took man's guilt and its penalty, and offered in man's behalf a complete sacrifice to God (HP 65).

He stood in the place where fallen man was to stand under the descending stroke of justice, and, innocent, he suffered for the guilty, in order that those who believe in him as their personal Saviour, should be accounted guiltless (THM, December 1, 1894).

Christ was treated as we deserve, that we might be treated as

He deserves. He was condemned for our sins, in which He had no share, that we might be justified by His righteousness, in which we had no share. He suffered the death which was ours, that we might receive the life which was His. "With His stripes we are healed" (DA 25).

Oh, how magnificent and wonderful is the gospel!

In the final analysis, it wasn't nails, thorns, or physical crucifixion that caused Jesus Christ's death. The Jews didn't kill Him, nor did the Romans. Neither was His demise simply the result of "natural consequences." Instead, Jesus' death was the result of a premeditated, well thought-out, divine act preplanned in eternity by the Father and the Son. Jesus died because of "our sins" (1 Corinthians 15:3), because a heavenly "sword" struck the sin that He bore. This is what ended His life—as it is written:

Yet it pleased *the* LORD to bruise Him;
He has put Him to grief (Isaiah 53:10; emphasis added).

This verse says that *God did it,* which is why He alone is responsible for our salvation.

Johnny's blood

In his book *Written in Blood,* Robert Coleman tells a story from long ago when doctors made house calls. Mary, a young girl, was lying on the verge of death because of a disease from which her older brother, Johnny, had recovered two years earlier. "Mary needs a blood transfusion quickly or she will die," the doctor told the parents, "and Johnny's blood is perfect because he has already conquered the disease."

All eyes turned toward Johnny. "Are you willing to give your blood?" the lad's parents tearfully asked him.

He hesitated for a moment. Then, his lower lip trembling, he replied, "Sure. She's my sister."

Upon his consent, they all rushed to the hospital. Soon, Johnny and Mary lay next to each other in the operating room. Johnny's body was healthy, while Mary's was pale and weak. Neither child spoke, but when their eyes met, Johnny grinned. Then tubes were connected, needles were inserted, and the red liquid began to flow.

When the transfusion was nearly complete, Johnny broke the silence by asking the doctor in a shaky voice, "When do I die?" Only then did the adults realize why the lad's lip had trembled when he agreed to donate his blood. He had thought that by transferring his blood, he was giving his life for her. Unselfishly, he had made the great decision because he loved his sister.

Our Messiah gave His life for us, a willing Substitute. Unlike Johnny, however, Jesus did have to die, for justice required it. Not just His Father's justice, but His own too—for remember, Jesus and His Father are One (John 10:30). This bears repeating. It wasn't the Father's justice alone that Jesus was mercifully satisfying. No! It was the eternal quality of absolute fairness firmly embedded in the characters of *both* of Them that was being wonderfully satisfied by Their joint act of total self-sacrifice. Why did They do it? The reason is simple: so that They could justly extend everlasting mercy to us! Permeating everything—including the sword—was Their mutual love for you and me. Yes, love did it. This is the greatest lesson of Calvary.

But how great was the cost! "From the sixth hour [noon] until the ninth hour [3:00 P.M.] there was darkness over all the land" (Matthew 27:45). There are deep places on ocean floors where light has never shined. Such darkness is comparable to what descended "over all the land" surrounding the Place of the Skull. Yet an even greater darkness settled upon the Man in the middle. "At the ninth hour the darkness lifted from the people, but still enveloped the Saviour. It was a symbol of the agony and horror that weighed upon His heart" (DA 754). Human beings will never fully understand this horror. It was the horror of separation, the nightmare of a razor-sharp "sword" slicing the unity of the divine Father and Son.

"About the ninth hour Jesus cried out with a loud voice, saying, 'Eli, Eli, lama sabachthani?' that is, 'My God, My God, why have You forsaken Me?' " (Matthew 27:46). Even in the darkest places along the bottom of earth's oceans, sea creatures yet live. But when "the guilt of every descendant of Adam" (DA 753) pressed upon Christ's heart, hardly anything could live, not even hope—the guilt was so dark and so deep. As we've seen, God hates evil with terrible passion, and at that time the totality of evil was inside His own Son! In the Father's heart, both love and hate clashed like titans. Who can fathom this struggle? Finally, during one awful moment, Christ felt forsaken. "Why?" He screamed into the sky. Because of sin and the sword. And so, two Lovers were ripped apart.

> The wrath of God against sin, the terrible manifestation of His displeasure because of iniquity, filled the soul of His Son with consternation. All His life Christ had been publishing to a fallen world the good news of the Father's mercy and pardoning love. Salvation for the chief of sinners was His theme. But now with the terrible weight of guilt He bears, He cannot see the Father's reconciling face. The withdrawal of the divine countenance from the Saviour in this hour of supreme anguish pierced His heart with a sorrow that can never be fully understood by man. So great was this agony that His physical pain was hardly felt (DA 753).

The paragraph above contains a good definition of the wrath of God. It is "the terrible manifestation of His displeasure because of iniquity." Yet again, in the deepest sense, what happened on Golgotha's rocky ridge was "a revelation of [God's] character of love" (COL 415). This can't be repeated too often. Love motivated the Godhead to offer this unfathomable sacrifice. Their joint pain and agony unveils Their holy heart.

A little boy who lived in a ghetto once grabbed the pant leg of a street preacher who was telling a crowd about God's love. "Mister," the kid declared, "I want to see love with skin on it!" On Calvary, our God revealed that very thing. He put human skin on His love—His *personal* love—for you and me.

A virtual feast

As we near the conclusion of this chapter, feast your eyes on this:

> The spotless Son of God hung upon the cross, His flesh lacerated with stripes; those hands so often reached out in blessing, nailed to the wooden bars; those feet so tireless on ministries of love, spiked to the tree; that royal head pierced by the crown of thorns; those quivering lips shaped to the cry of woe. And all that He endured—the blood drops that flowed from His head, His

hands, His feet, the agony that wracked His frame, and the unutterable anguish that filled His soul at the hiding of His Father's face—speaks to each child of humanity, declaring, It is for thee that the Son of God consents to bear this burden of guilt; for thee He spoils the domain of death, and opens the gates of Paradise. He who stilled the angry waves and walked the foam-capped billows, who made devils tremble and disease flee, who opened blind eyes and called forth the dead to life,—offers Himself upon the cross as a sacrifice, and this from love to thee. He, the Sin Bearer, endures the wrath of divine justice, and for thy sake becomes sin itself (DA 755, 756).

Here are all the elements: Jesus, "the Sin Bearer"; "the wrath of divine justice"; and an unspeakable sacrifice motivated by "love to thee."

Let's summarize what we've learned. First, God can't overlook any sin *ever*—from the time of Adam to the end. We know this because *every sin* was transferred to Jesus in Gethsemane and on the cross. This reveals His uncompromising justice.

Second, our God is good! That hill far away reveals a loving Creator who willingly and graciously humbled Himself, became a man, became our Substitute, took our sins, bore our guilt, and died in our place to save us. This shows His incredible love and mercy.

Third, His plan is perfect. Angels marvel and stoop low to see it played out.

Fourth, if we fail to grasp this exquisite interplay between impartial justice and costly mercy, we've missed the boat entirely and can never really understand either the true character of God or the real gospel of Jesus Christ.

Justice and Mercy stood apart, in opposition to each other, separated by a wide gulf. The Lord our Redeemer clothed His divinity with humanity, and wrought out in behalf of man a character that was without spot or blemish. He planted His cross midway between heaven and earth, and made it the object of attraction which reached both ways, drawing both Justice and Mercy across the gulf. Justice moved from its exalted throne, and with all the armies of heaven approached the cross. There it saw

> One equal with God bearing the penalty for all injustice and sin. With perfect satisfaction Justice bowed in reverence at the cross, saying, It is enough (7 SDABC 936).

Hallelujah—it's enough! During those final seconds before His death between two thieves, hope returned to Christ's suffering heart. Relying by faith on the "sure word of prophecy" (2 Peter 1:19, KJV) that He would be resurrected and on His Father's love, Jesus triumphantly shouted, " 'It is finished' " (John 19:30). Then He bowed His head and died.

> Amid the awful darkness, apparently forsaken of God, Christ had drained the last dregs in the cup of human woe. In those dreadful hours He had relied upon the evidence of His Father's acceptance heretofore given Him. He was acquainted with the character of His Father; He understood His justice, His mercy, and His great love. By faith He rested in Him whom it had ever been His joy to obey. And as in submission He committed Himself to God, the sense of the loss of His Father's favor was withdrawn. By faith, Christ was victor (DA 756).

Now contemplate this: "The unconverted man thinks of God as unloving, as severe, and even revengeful. . . . But when Jesus is seen upon the cross, as the gift of God because He loved man, the eyes are opened to see things in a new light. God as revealed in Christ is not a severe judge, an avenging tyrant, but a merciful and loving Father" (1 SM 183).

This is who God really is. It is only in the light that streams from the Place of the Skull that we can we truly "see Him as He is" (1 John 3:2). Incredibly, when we behold our Maker in this light, even the sword of justice flashes encouragingly.

Think of it this way: God has already dealt with every sin you have ever committed. He has fully satisfied His own justice. In God's Son your sins met His sword and lost. Overflowing mercy now beckons. How you respond to God's goodness is up to you.

---

1. James Strong, *The New Strong's Dictionary of Hebrew and Greek Words* (Nashville: Thomas Nelson, 1996), s.v. "chereb"; emphasis in the original.

2. *Merriam-Webster Online Dictionary*, s.v. "justice," http://www

.merriam-webster.com/justice (accessed June 12, 2008).

3. W. E. Vine, Merrill F. Unger, and William White Jr., *Vine's Complete Expository Dictionary of Old and New Testament Words* (Nashville: Thomas Nelson, 1996), s.v. "akratos."

4. James Strong, *The New Strong's Dictionary of Hebrew and Greek Words* (Nashville: Thomas Nelson, 1996), s.v. "akratos."

5. James Strong, *The Exhaustive Concordance of the Bible: Showing Every Word of the Text of the Common English Version of the Canonical Books, and Every Occurrence of Each Word in Regular Order,* electronic edition (Elmira, Ontario: Woodside Bible Fellowship, 1996), s.v. "akratos."

For Further Thought and Discussion

1. Why did the Son of God stagger and almost collapse as He approached the Garden of Gethsemane with His disciples?
2. In Gethsemane, Christ "saw what justice meant" (DA 686). What does justice mean?
3. Describe as best you can the interplay between justice and mercy in Christ's garden conflict.
4. Explain how Gethsemane and Calvary help us to understand God's character in a new way—to see with new eyes.
5. Can becoming parents help us to appreciate better the Gethsemane conflict? How?
6. Why should the Cross be the supreme center of the Christian life?
7. Why is it so easy for us to blame God for our problems instead of blaming either Satan or sin?
8. Is God ever really to blame for anything?
9. Explain how what happened on the cross vindicates God's justice, manifests His mercy, and reveals His loving heart.
10. What impressed you the most in this chapter, and why?

CHAPTER 7

THE RIGHTEOUSNESS OF JESUS CHRIST

Among the attributes of God, although they are equal,
mercy shines with even more brilliancy than justice.

—Miguel de Cervantes

My family lives in the mountains of Auberry, California, just east of Fresno, about an hour from Yosemite National Park. Our house, nestled at the end of a dirt road, is rather isolated, which we appreciate. It's quiet, safe, and a wonderful place to raise kids. But recently something occurred that jarred our comfort. At six forty-five one evening, the power went out, and we unexpectedly found ourselves in pitch darkness.

"I have a prayer request," three-year-old Seth blurted out as we huddled together on our living room couch, holding flashlights. Dropping to his knees, he said, "Dear Jesus, please turn on the power so we can see. In Jesus' name. Amen." Then he opened his eyes, looked around, and blurted out, "Daddy, the power is still out!"

"Give Jesus some time," I replied calmly. "He doesn't always answer our prayers right away. Be patient."

Because Seth was frightened by the total blackness, our family all slept in one room that night. At 9:00 P.M. we still had no power. At 10:00 P.M. there was no change. Around midnight, I heard the heater start up, so I knew the power was restored. Then, at about a quarter after six, Seth jumped out of bed and began looking for one of his toys. "I need the flashlight," he whispered.

"Just turn on the light," I replied with a sleepy grin.

He did, and I love his response. "Whoa!" he said with a huge smile, "Jesus answered my prayer!"

I know this is a rather down-to-earth story, but the spiritual condition of our twenty-first-century world is a lot like the little town of Auberry on that dark Tuesday night. "Darkness shall cover the earth," prophecy predicted, "and deep darkness the people" (Isaiah 60:2). At no time in history is this truer than now, in these last days. Yet prophecy not only depicts darkness, but it also predicts an end-time burst of magnificent light all over the world. Those who see this light and who grasp its significance will say "Whoa!" just as Seth did when he flicked that switch at 6:15 A.M. Heaven's "power" will be turned on full force. Here's the prediction: "After these things I saw another angel coming down from heaven, having great authority, and the earth was illuminated with his glory" (Revelation 18:1).

This text describes a manifestation of heavenly light so mighty that planet Earth will be spiritually illuminated by its iridescent glory. We now know that God's glory is His character (see chapter 1). The following insightful commentary fits perfectly.

> It is the darkness of misapprehension of God that is enshrouding the world. Men are losing their knowledge of His character. It has been misunderstood and misinterpreted. At this time a message from God is to be proclaimed, a message illuminating in its influence and saving in its power. His character is to be made known. Into the darkness of the world is to be shed the light of His glory, the light of His goodness, mercy, and truth. . . .
>
> . . . The last rays of merciful light, the last message of mercy to be given to the world, is a revelation of His character of love (COL 415).

Significantly, this paragraph connects the "revelation of His character of love" with "a message from God . . . a message illuminating in its influence and saving in its power."

Now, compare those sentences above with these additional ones from the same pen.

> *The message of Christ's righteousness* is to sound from one end of the earth to the other to prepare the way of the Lord. This is the glory of God, which closes the work of the third angel (6T 19; emphasis added).

The time of test is just upon us, for the loud cry of the third angel has already begun in *the revelation of the righteousness of Christ,* the sin-pardoning Redeemer. This is the beginning of the light of the angel whose glory shall fill the whole earth (1 SM 363; emphasis added).

One interest will prevail, one subject will swallow up every other,—*Christ our righteousness* (RH, December 23, 1890; emphasis added).

When we put these pieces together, we discover that the message about God's "character of love" is inseparably connected with "the message of Christ's righteousness." Neither message should replace the other. Just as the Father and His Son are One in character, even so should the character of God message and the righteousness of Jesus Christ message become one too. Like twin rails on a train track, they can't be separated. If we split them up or try riding only one rail, we may miss our trip to heaven.

Jesus' righteousness and the law

Next point: there is also an inseparable connection between the righteousness of Jesus Christ message and the law of God. Shortly, I will prove this from the Bible. Lucifer hates this connection, but we must get it if we are to ever comprehend the Lord's final message to a dying world.

"There is much light yet to shine forth from the law of God and the gospel of righteousness. This message, understood in its true character, and proclaimed in the Spirit, will lighten the earth with its glory" (1888 166).

If we would have the spirit and power of the third angel's message, we must present the law and the gospel together, for they go hand in hand. As a power from beneath is stirring up the children of disobedience to make void the law of God, and to trample upon the truth that Christ is our righteousness, a power from above is moving upon the hearts of those who are loyal, to exalt the law, and to lift up Jesus as a complete Saviour (GW 161, 162).

About 120 years ago, in 1888, a unique Seventh-day Adventist General Conference Session took place in Minneapolis, Minnesota. Among the delegates were two young ministers from California, Ellet J. Waggoner and Alonzo T. Jones. On that historic occasion, these two men gave a series of Bible studies that focused especially on the righteousness of Christ as taught by Paul in the books of Romans and Galatians. Ellen White was there, listening intently. She later reflected that at the conference itself and shortly thereafter, "Elder E. J. Waggoner had the privilege granted him of speaking plainly and presenting his views upon justification by faith and the righteousness of Christ in relation to the law" (3 SM 168). "I see the beauty of truth in the presentation of the righteousness of Christ in relation to the law as the doctor [E. J. Waggoner] has placed it before us" (1888 164).

When I was a child growing up in Studio City, California, I loved jigsaw puzzles. Hour after hour I sat on the floor of our home putting the pieces together. Sometimes the puzzle image was a house, an animal, or some nature scene. For the past twenty-eight years, since I became a Christian, I've been doing something similar—trying to figure out, piece by piece, text by text, and quote by quote, the true message of Jesus Christ for these last days. When I put the quotations above from Ellen G. White together, the pieces fit perfectly. Light flashes. Darkness is dispelled. God's person, His character, His love, His law, and His gospel all go together. Believe it or not, if we have spiritual discernment, we can find all of these heavenly elements within one Bible text. That verse reads, "Here is the patience of the saints; here are those who keep the *commandments* of *God* and the *faith* of *Jesus*" (Revelation 14:12; emphasis added). The focus of this apocalyptic passage is "God," His "commandments," "faith," and above all, "Jesus." Exactly how do these puzzle pieces fit together? Let me explain.

Paul wrote, "The law was our schoolmaster to bring us unto Christ, that we might be justified by faith" (Galatians 3:24, KJV). According to this verse, one of the primary functions of "the law" is to serve as "our schoolmaster to bring us unto Christ." The way it does this is by revealing two things: (1) the attributes of God's character, which show His perfect will for our lives, and (2) how miserably we have fallen short.

If we are honest with our own hearts, it's not difficult to see. Just open your Bible to Exodus 20:3–17, say a sincere prayer for the enlightenment of the Holy Spirit, and then slowly, carefully, and reverently *read the Ten Commandments*. When we do this, the Holy Spirit enables us to discern how many times we have

- failed to put God first,
- embraced false gods (including false mental pictures of God),
- dishonored His holy name both in speech and in life,
- broken the Sabbath,
- dishonored our parents,
- practiced murder or self-murder or hate,
- yielded to sexual impurity,
- rejected strict honesty,
- lied about others,
- and not been content with what we have.

Both the Old and New Testaments teach that the Ten Commandments can be succinctly summarized in two great commandments: we are to love God with all our heart, soul, mind, and strength, and we are to love our neighbors as ourselves (see Leviticus 19:18; Deuteronomy 6:5; Matthew 22:34–40). Thus it is love—unselfish, sacrificial love—that is the essence of God's law (see Romans 13:10). It must be so, because "God is love" (1 John 4:8), and because such love is the heart of who He is.

In the penetrating light of God's holy, pure, and supremely unselfish law of love, it should be quite obvious that all of us "fall short of the glory [character] of God" (Romans 3:23). Seeing this contrast between what God is like and what we are like naturally troubles our consciences. It gives us a deep, searing sense that we have done something horrible; we have failed our Maker. It doesn't matter what religion we profess, whether Christian, Jewish, Muslim, New Age, Wiccan, or Hindu, or whether we've professed no religion at all, an honest look at the "big ten" accompanied by the convicting power of the Holy Spirit will create guilt in our hearts. And more than this, it will automatically make us realize that we need a Savior. This is how "the law" becomes "our schoolmaster to bring us unto Christ."

"When the law was proclaimed from Sinai, God made known to men the holiness of His character, that by contrast they might see the sinfulness of their own. The law was given to convict them of sin, and reveal their need of a Saviour. It would do this as its principles were applied to the heart by the Holy Spirit. *This work it is still to do"* (DA 308).

Thus the Bible combines bad news with good news. The bad news is that—in the light of God's law—we are all lost sinners. But then comes the good news: we have a Savior! Motivated by the attributes of His unselfish character, the Lord has graciously provided a way out—a way that maintains His justice and yet manifests His mercy. But it is right here that Lucifer often steps in to upset God's plan and to bring in confusion. Notice carefully: "But it is ever the purpose of Satan to make void the law of God and to pervert the true meaning of the plan of salvation" (FW 118). It is our task to detect and reject his satanic wiles.

Extremes abound

Because of devilish subtlety, extremes abound, even in the religious world. Today, many Christians speak lovingly of Jesus but reject His law. Others coldly stress the importance of obedience to God's commandments, but their hearts are devoid of sunshine, kindness, and grace. Still others seek to promote what they perceive as "the true character of God," yet they don't talk much about the authority of the Ten Commandments, the reality of personal guilt, or the solemnity of the day of judgment. In the latter case, all too often, "love is dwelt upon as the chief attribute of God, but it is degraded to a weak sentimentalism, making little distinction between good and evil. God's justice, His denunciations of sin, the requirements of His holy law, are all kept out of sight" (GC 558).

This is not genuine love, but "weak sentimentalism." True love will maintain "the requirements of [God's] holy law." The Lord doesn't change; His standards of right and wrong are solid, fixed, and unbending. The happiness and eternal security of the entire universe depends on this. But oh! God's love is solid, fixed, and unbending too, and He has developed a costly rescue plan perfectly consistent with *all* of His royal attributes. The living Center of this plan is His Son. An Old Testament prophecy about Jesus predicted, " 'This is His name by which He will be called: THE LORD OUR RIGHTEOUSNESS' " (Jeremiah 23:6).

What does it mean that Jesus Christ is "our righteousness"? We must discover the answer, because hidden within this text and terminology lies God's last message for a dying world. Let's tackle it, especially in the context of God's character.

In its simplest terms, "righteousness is right doing" (COL 312), which means doing what is right because it is right. Contrary to Satan's accusations, our Creator is a righteous God—which means that He does the right thing 100 percent of the time. Again, the loyal universe depends on this. On Mount Sinai, God used His holy finger to write the eternal principles of His righteousness in solid rock. The Bible frequently connects the word *righteousness* with the law. Notice, for instance, "all Your commandments are righteousness" (Psalm 119:172), "the righteousness of the law" (Romans 2:26; 8:4, KJV), and "the law of righteousness" (Romans 9:31, KJV).

Pretty plain isn't it? Scripturally speaking, *righteousness* is defined by God's law. The following statements simply agree with the Word.

> Righteousness is defined by the standard of God's holy law, as expressed in the ten precepts given on Sinai (SC 61).

> Righteousness can be defined only by God's great moral standard, the Ten Commandments (ST, June 20, 1895).

> The law is the great standard of righteousness (CT 62).

That makes it doubly plain. Now let's notice again the relationship between the law and sin. First, from Scripture,

> Moses said to the people [after they heard the Ten Commandments], "Do not fear; for God has come to test you, and that His fear may be before you, so that you may not sin" (Exodus 20:20).

> By the law is the knowledge of sin (Romans 3:20).

> If you really fulfill the royal law according to the Scripture, "You shall love your neighbor as yourself," you do well; but if you show partiality, you commit sin, and are convicted by the law as transgressors (James 2:8, 9).

> Whosoever committeth sin transgresseth also the law: for sin is the transgression of the law (1 John 3:4, KJV).

Now for additional support.

Sin is defined to be "the transgression of the law." 1 John 3:5, 4 (COL 311).

Teach the youth that sin in any line is defined in the Scriptures as "transgression of the law." 1 John 3:4 (CT 169).

Our only definition of sin is that given in the word of God; it is "the transgression of the law" (GC 493).

Now it's triply plain—but we're not done yet! If God is a righteous God, and if His law is a transcript of His righteous character, and if sin is biblically defined as breaking His law, then what does it mean that Jesus Christ has become "the Lord *our* righteousness"?

Here's the answer: as the royal Man among men, Jesus Christ flawlessly and unselfishly obeyed the Ten Commandments *in human flesh throughout His entire life in our behalf* through faith in His Father. Near the end of His earthly life, Christ stated with absolute innocence, " 'I have kept My Father's commandments and abide in His love' " (John 15:10). By obeying the "big ten" in human flesh—that is, by living a life of unselfish love for both God and human beings—day by day, step by step, and test by test, the Son of God earned the right to receive the prophetic name "the Lord our righteousness."

Again, it's obvious that we each have failed miserably. We've been selfish, loveless, proud, and disobedient—in a nutshell, we have become quite Luciferian. Originally created in God's image, we now most often reflect the devil. How many Bible verses do we need to shatter our cozy complacency and to convince us of our true condition? Two texts from Romans 3 should be sufficient: " 'There is none righteous, no not one' " (verse 10). "All have sinned and fall short of the glory of God" (verse 23).

That's the bad news: we have broken God's law. But, ah—thank God for the good news! Jesus kept the law perfectly in our behalf! Not only that, but at the end of thirty-three years of righteous living in human flesh, Jesus took another preordained, fearful "step." Plunge is more accurate. While lying face down beneath the olive trees in a lonely garden, Jesus made the calculated but fearful choice to take our sins, bear our guilt, feel the sword, taste the full penalty of a broken law, and ultimately die the death that God's broken law requires *of us* as lawbreakers! He was separated from His Father—yet They were willing to go through this because of Their unfathomable, intense love for us. Because of these fearful and joyful realities, Jesus can now legitimately forgive our sins, lift our guilt, and impute to us His own spotless righteousness as a gift. *This is the plan of salvation that God—in harmony with His character— has painstakingly devised for our redemption.* It maintains His justice, yet allows Him to manifest His mercy toward the lost—toward you and me.

What about our response?

Now let's get practical. We've seen what Jesus did, but what about us? What should we do? John the Baptist thundered, " 'Repent!' " (Matthew 3:2). Likewise, Jesus Himself also proclaimed that we should repent (see Mark 1:15). Peter even declared that true repentance—which means giving up sin because we see how hateful it is—is a gift (see Acts 5:31). It comes from God. And Paul taught " 'repentance toward God and faith toward our Lord Jesus Christ' " (Acts 20:21).

In the book of Romans, Paul also wrote of the supreme importance of "faith in his blood" (Romans 3:25, KJV). Yet many today have lost sight of the necessity of repentance, faith in Christ, and the idea of trusting the merits of our Savior's blood. There's a reason for this: Lucifer is at work behind the scenes. But "the true religion, the only religion of the Bible" still teaches "the forgiveness of sins, the righteousness of Christ, and the blood of the Lamb" (1888 948).

As we've already seen, "the righteousness of Christ" is the righteous character that Jesus Christ developed during His earthly sojourn by keeping the Ten Commandments in our behalf. His righteous life met the law's requirements perfectly. More than this, Christ's righteousness is the *only* righteousness that meets those requirements, which makes it our only hope of heaven. This is the true reason why "one interest will prevail, one subject will swallow up every other,—Christ our righteousness" (RH, December 23, 1890).

Here is how Paul so masterfully put these pieces together in the book of Romans: "Now we know that whatever the law says, it says to those who are under the law, that every mouth may be stopped, and all the world may become guilty before God. Therefore by the deeds of the law no flesh will be justified in His sight, for by the law is the knowledge of sin" (Romans 3:19, 20). In other words, Paul argues that in the penetrating light of God's law, all the world is guilty before God. Many refuse to accept this, but their reasoning is futile. "You are guilty!" is still the verdict of Heaven.

Now here's a vital point. Because all the world stands guilty before God, nobody can be justified, or made not guilty, by his or her efforts to keep the law. Imagine a murderer who, after sitting reflectively in jail for half a year, petitions his judge, "Your Honor, I've been a nice guy for six months now! Won't you justify me?" The answer is obvious—not a chance! The same is true of us. When we've broken God's law, that law can only condemn us, it can't justify us or save us. On the contrary, "by the law is the knowledge of sin"—that is, the only thing we can get from the law is the uncompromising message that we are utterly lost, helpless, undone, and condemned. "The whole world stands condemned before the great moral standard of righteousness" (ST, March 7, 1895).

If there were no "rest of the story," there would be no need to write this book. However, Paul continued, "But now the righteousness of God [which is the only righteousness the Lord will accept] apart from the law [meaning that it comes from somewhere other than the law] is revealed" (Romans 3:21). Where is this essential righteousness revealed? In Jesus Christ.

Now here's the great news. This "righteousness of God" is now freely offered to every sinner "through faith in Jesus Christ" (verse 22). In other words, if we repent of our sins and have simple faith in Jesus as "the Lord *our* righteousness," then God will justify us freely, forgive our sins, and boldly pronounce us not guilty before His entire universe! The following paragraph explains this perfectly.

> It was possible for Adam, before the fall, to form a righteous character by obedience to God's law. But he failed to do this, and because of his sin our natures are fallen and we cannot make ourselves righteous. Since we are sinful, unholy, we cannot perfectly obey the holy law. We have no righteousness of our own with which to meet the claims of the law of God. But Christ has made a way of escape for us. He lived on earth amid trials and temptations such as we have to meet. He lived a sinless life. He died for us, and now He offers to take our sins and give us His

righteousness. If you give yourself to Him, and accept Him as your Saviour, then, sinful as your life may have been, for His sake you are accounted righteous. Christ's character stands in place of your character, and you are accepted before God just as if you had not sinned (SC 62).

Another controversy

What a message! Yet a great controversy rages around these biblical truths. Some believe that God is so good that He will accept us even if we don't firmly rely on the righteousness of Jesus Christ. Or they interpret the phrase *His righteousness* as meaning merely that God is right and loving in a general (and often vague) sense. To those who believe this, the transaction described above in which Jesus Christ "offers to take our sins and give us His righteousness" so that we are then "accounted righteous" becomes virtually meaningless.

Some even argue that all such legal transaction terminology is problematic in itself, that it merely reflects "a legal model" that doesn't accurately present the true character of God. According to this perspective, the very idea of "accounted righteousness" is fictitious. Various theories are now being put forth to explain exactly how this erroneous legal terminology somehow worked its way into the Bible, but the conclusion is usually the same: that what the Bible says (and what Ellen White wrote in her careful commentary) is not to be taken literally.

Honestly, we believe that this "it's only a legal model" theory is *extremely dangerous* because it effectively undermines—in one sweep—the entire fabric of what biblical righteousness by faith is all about. The sentence from the book *Steps to Christ* quoted above that states, "Christ's character stands in place of your character, and you are accepted before God just as if you had not sinned," does in fact teach that Christians will experience a change in legal status. Its context is "the claims of the law of God" that were met by our Savior, who alone "lived a sinless life." Does God's law really have claims upon us? Yes, it does—because it is connected to His justice. Were such claims actually satisfied by Jesus Christ? Indeed, and this is the genuine outworking of His mercy. It's all part of the royal plan—which Lucifer hates!

Let's go back to Scripture. Paul wrote about "the blessedness of the man to whom God imputes righteousness apart from works" (Romans

4:6). The Greek word translated "imputes" is *logizomai. Vine's Complete Expository Dictionary of Old and New Testament Words* says that this word "primarily signifies 'to reckon,' whether by calculation or imputation."[1] Strong's exhaustive concordance says "to pass to one's account, to impute."[2] Thus God will "impute," or "reckon" to our "account," "righteousness apart from works." Whose righteousness? Paul's answer is *the righteousness of Jesus Christ.* In other words, we have no righteousness of our own to meet the just claims of God's law, but if we will surrender our hearts to Jesus and trust Him as our Savior, then God will graciously apply thirty-three years of His own Son's righteous living to our personal account in the books of record.

Notice carefully Ellen White's commentary on Romans 4:5. I pray that as you read it, the Holy Spirit will impress you that this is not just fictitious legal terminology, but the living truth of God now being revealed for our salvation.

> Righteousness is obedience to the law. The law demands righteousness, and this the sinner owes to the law; but he is incapable of rendering it. The only way in which he can attain to righteousness is through faith. *By faith he can bring to God the merits of Christ, and the Lord places the obedience of His Son to the sinner's account.* Christ's righteousness is accepted in place of man's failure, and God receives, pardons, justifies, the repentant, believing soul, treats him as though he were righteous, and loves him as He loves His Son. *This is how faith is accounted righteousness* (FW 101; emphasis added).

The Bible itself says that Jesus Christ's righteousness is imputed to us "by faith." Paul focused on "the righteousness of God, through faith in Jesus Christ" (Romans 3:22). This kind of faith does not mean a mere mental assent to doctrinal truth, nor does it mean simply the acknowledging of God's goodness. Rather, it is a fully submissive, heart-surrendering faith that has not only been deeply penetrated by Christ's matchless charms and tender love, but that is directed toward the Savior for a purpose—to lay hold of His righteousness. Such "faith seizes and appropriates the righteousness of Christ" (1888 373). It also deeply appreciates the merits of His blood.

Paul affirmed, "We have redemption through His blood, the forgiveness of sins" (Ephesians 1:7). The book of Revelation also testifies to the significance, power, and cleansing virtue of the blood of our Savior, speaking of "Him who loved us and washed us from our sins in His own blood" (chapter 1:5) and of the saints, who " 'overcame him [the devil] by the blood of the Lamb and by the word of their testimony' " (chapter 12:11). Thus, the blood of Jesus Christ is a central issue in the character of God controversy.

In a nutshell, Christ's blood represents His worthiness—the merits of His righteousness. We broke the law, but Jesus didn't. We've sinned, but Christ committed " 'no sin' " (1 Peter 2:22). On the Day of Atonement, the blood of the sacrifice was sprinkled above the mercy seat seven times (Leviticus 16:14). Moses told the Israelites this was done to " 'make atonement for you, to cleanse you, that you may be clean from all your sins before the LORD' " (Leviticus 16:30). This verse does not reflect fictitious legal terminology, but the living truth of God. That ancient act lay at the heart of the entire sanctuary service. It speaks to us today.

Within God's last day message,

> *The efficacy of the blood of Christ [must] be presented to the people with freshness and power, that their faith might lay hold upon its merits.* As the high priest sprinkled the warm blood upon the mercy seat, while the fragrant cloud of incense ascended before God, so while we confess our sins and plead the efficacy of Christ's atoning blood, our prayers are to ascend to heaven, fragrant with the merits of our Saviour's character. Notwithstanding our unworthiness, we are ever to bear in mind that there is One that can take away sin and save the sinner. Every sin acknowledged before God with a contrite heart, He will remove. *This faith is the life of the church* (TM 92, 93; emphasis added).

Both just and justifier

Of deep significance is the scripture that says that God "set forth [Jesus] as a propitiation by His blood . . . that He might be *just* and the *justifier* of the one who has faith in Jesus" (Romans 3:25, 26; emphasis added). This is the epitome of Paul's arguments in Romans 1–3 and demonstrates how the biblical message of righteousness by faith in Jesus

Christ is truly an ingeniously devised plan formulated and skillfully implemented by both the Father and the Son, a plan that not only defends Their nonnegotiable attribute of infinite justice but also legitimizes what They desire most—to grant mercy to us. "Glorious truth!—just to His own law, and yet the Justifier of all that believe in Jesus" (MB 116).

We must understand this: God is so just that He cannot ignore, overlook, or excuse any violations of His law. He will " 'by no means' " (Exodus 34:7) clear the guilty. Yet His justice, while firmly rooted in His uncompromising commitment to righteousness—to what is right—is inseparably intertwined with His love for the lost. And so, compelled by this love, two thousand years ago He amazingly and unselfishly chose to lay aside His divinity and be made flesh (which is comparable to a human being becoming an ant) for the specific purpose of forming a righteous character in behalf of those who have no righteousness of their own. Then He died for our sins and rose from the dead, and now He offers to take our sins and give us His righteousness. If we respond to such love, repent of our sins, and trust Jesus as our Savior, He doesn't simply clear the guilty. Instead, He removes our guilt entirely and treats us as if we never sinned! This is how guilty lawbreakers like us can legitimately be justified by faith, and how God's gracious character shines forth as the sun.

"The moment the sinner believes in Christ, he stands in the sight of God uncondemned; for the righteousness of Christ is his: Christ's perfect obedience is imputed to him" (FCE 430). "The Lord imputes unto the believer the righteousness of Christ and pronounces him righteous before the universe. He transfers his sins to Jesus, the sinner's representative, substitute, and surety" (1 SM 392).

However, the effect of this good news reaches far beyond forgiveness. When we trust Jesus fully, He "changes the heart" (SC 62). Such a change is absolutely necessary because, from God's perspective, our natural heart is like a corroded battery that must be replaced. Or, to use a medical illustration, our spiritual hearts are 100 percent saturated with spiritual cholesterol, with every artery blocked. Apart from the gospel, there's no cure. Our only hope is a divine operation performed by the Great Physician. A quadruple bypass won't do. We need a heart transplant from a heavenly Donor. When we fully submit to Jesus' gracious touch, He changes us on the inside. " 'I will give you a new heart' " is His promise

(Ezekiel 36:26). We must trust Him for this. He has never lost a case. As the famous hymn, "Rock of Ages," says, "Nothing in my hands I bring, simply to the cross I cling." Jesus loves us, and those who come to Him He will in " 'no means cast out' " (John 6:37).

There's more! The complete message of the righteousness of Jesus Christ advances even beyond forgiveness and a new heart. Its ultimate goal is not just imputed righteousness to cover our past sins, but also imparted righteousness—which is spiritual power—to bring us back into harmony with the law of God. *This was the message preached by A. T. Jones and E. J. Waggoner in 1888.* Of all of Ellen White's post-1888 descriptions of that message, the following paragraph is the most comprehensive. Read it carefully.

> The Lord in His great mercy sent a most precious message to His people through Elders [E. J.] Waggoner and [A. T.] Jones. This message was to bring more prominently before the world the uplifted Saviour, the sacrifice for the sins of the whole world. It presented justification through faith in the Surety [imputed righteousness]; it invited the people to receive the righteousness of Christ [imparted righteousness], which is made manifest in obedience to all the commandments of God. Many had lost sight of Jesus. They needed to have their eyes directed to His divine person, His merits, and His changeless love for the human family. All power is given into His hands, that He may dispense rich gifts unto men, imparting the priceless gift of His own righteousness to the helpless human agent. *This is the message that God commanded to be given to the world. It is the third angel's message, which is to be proclaimed with a loud voice, and attended with the outpouring of His Spirit in a large measure* (TM 91, 92; emphasis added).

There it is—God's true, end-time, apocalyptic message based on the Bible. It exalts Jesus Christ, His love, His sacrifice, His blood, His merits, His righteousness, and His divine power to enable us to keep His law; which, again, is simply a transcript of His character. Thus this entire message reveals what God is really like. He is our Creator, Ruler, Lawgiver, Redeemer, Justifier, Sanctifier, and above all, the Supreme Lover of our souls, who has made an infinite sacrifice to save us from sin. Yet hiding within shadows, even inside the church, is our ancient enemy, who hates who God really is and these truths—every one of them. Look closely.

The thought that the righteousness of Christ is imputed to us, not because of any merit on our part, but as a free gift from God, is a precious thought. *The enemy of God and man is not willing that this truth should be clearly presented; for he knows that if the people receive it fully, his power will be broken* (GW 161; emphasis added).

"The law was our schoolmaster to bring us unto Christ, that we might be justified by faith" (Gal. 3:24). In this scripture, the Holy Spirit through the apostle is speaking especially of the moral law. The law reveals sin to us, and causes us to feel our need of Christ and to flee unto Him for pardon and peace by exercising repentance toward God and faith toward our Lord Jesus Christ.

An unwillingness to yield up preconceived opinions, and to accept *this truth,* lay at the foundation of a large share of the opposition manifested at Minneapolis against the Lord's message through Brethren [E. J.] Waggoner and [A.T.] Jones. By exciting that opposition *Satan succeeded* in shutting away from our people, in a great measure, the special power of the Holy Spirit that God longed to impart to them. *The enemy* prevented them from obtaining that efficiency which might have been theirs in carrying the truth to the world, as the apostles proclaimed it after the day of Pentecost. The light that is to lighten the whole earth with its glory was resisted, and by the action of our own brethren has been in a great degree kept away from the world (1 SM 234, 235; emphasis added).

Lucifer is so subtle that he will " 'deceive, if possible, even the elect' " (Matthew 24:24). In these last days it is even possible for him to war against the message of the righteousness of Jesus Christ under the guise of promoting "the true character of God." He did the same thing in heaven. Working with "mysterious secrecy," the devil "concealed his real purpose under an appearance of reverence for God" (PP 37). But it was all a trick. By that time, Satan had no real reverence for his Maker. Instead, he hated Him. And his deceptions were so subtle that even holy angels were misled. This should put us all on our toes! Truly, we must stick to the Word of God rather than human opinions, however sweet those opinions may sound.

As we conclude this chapter, we are now fully prepared to understand the connection between these inspiring statements:

> The time of test is just upon us, for the loud cry of the third angel has already begun in the revelation of the righteousness of Christ, the sin-pardoning Redeemer. This is the beginning of the light of the angel whose glory shall fill the whole earth [Rev. 18:1] (RH, November 22, 1892).

> The message of Christ's righteousness is to sound from one end of the earth to the other to prepare the way of the Lord. This is the glory of God, which closes the work of the third angel (6T 19).

> The last rays of merciful light, the last message of mercy to be given to the world, is a revelation of His character of love (COL 415).

While driving along Interstate 99 recently, en route to Grandma's house, my family recently witnessed another one of God's gorgeous sunsets. Its last rays shone exquisitely, and then they were gone. Dear friend, just as a setting sun casts its fading beams before night settles, even so is Jesus Christ now sending His "last rays of merciful light" into our hearts before the end of the world (Matthew 24:14). Let's respond to His gracious offer while there's still time.

---

1. W. E. Vine, Merrill F. Unger, and William White Jr., *Vine's Complete Expository Dictionary of Old and New Testament Words* (Nashville: Thomas Nelson, 1996), s.v. "logizomai."

2. James Strong, *The Exhaustive Concordance of the Bible: Showing Every Word of the Text of the Common English Version of the Canonical Books, and Every Occurrence of Each Word in Regular Order,* electronic edition (Ontario: Woodside Bible Fellowship, 1996), s.v. "logizomai."

For Further Thought and Discussion

1. Practically speaking, what do you think will happen when Revelation 18:1 is completely fulfilled?
2. What could be hindering the fulfillment of this prophecy right now?
3. This chapter shows the relationship between the message of God's character and the message of Christ's righteousness. How are they related?
4. What is the difference between the righteousness of Christ imputed and the righteousness of Christ imparted?
5. Read Revelation 12:11 and then explain the significance of the blood of the Lamb.
6. Why is it difficult for many to understand the biblical message of righteousness by faith?
7. Why is righteousness by faith so encouraging?
8. How has Satan attacked and perverted the message of Jesus Christ's righteousness?
9. Suggest some practical ways in which we can share this message with others today.
10. What impressed you the most in this chapter, and why?

CHAPTER 8

WHEN MERCY CEASES

There is a time, we know not when,
A point we know not where,
That marks the destiny of men
To glory or despair.
There is a line by us unseen
That crosses every path,
The hidden boundary between
God's patience and His wrath.

—Joseph Addison Alexander

The story is told of an atheist university professor who boldly denied the validity of religion before his class. "Students," the man proudly announced, "God doesn't exist!" To prove his theory, he proposed an experiment. "I'm going to start this stopwatch," he said, "and then for the next sixty seconds I will curse any supposed deity in the sky and challenge him to strike me dead if he truly exists. Just watch; nothing will happen. This will prove God doesn't exist."

The class watched breathlessly as the godless professor pushed the button to start the stopwatch and then screamed, ranted, raved, cursed, mocked, and swore at the Creator of the universe, challenging Him to defend Himself and strike him dead if He could.

Nothing happened during those sixty seconds. Heaven made no response.

"You see!" proclaimed the professor gleefully. "This proves I'm right. God doesn't exist!"

But as most heads nodded agreement, a Christian seated at the back of the classroom whispered to his friend, "How tragic! Our teacher thinks he can exhaust the patience of God in only sixty seconds."

It's true. Jesus is infinitely more patient than humans can comprehend. For days, weeks, months, and years, even for thousands of years, He has graciously ministered to fallen men and women—even to those who hate Him. In spite of malignant evil, the Lord still " 'sends rain on the just and on the unjust' " (Matthew 5:45). Heaven's Ruler is a "God of patience" (Romans 15:5). He is "slow to anger, and abounding in mercy" (Psalm 103:8).

When Jesus gazes upon planet Earth, the sight must break His heart, for He beholds an endless stream of horrific sins, persistent rebellion, and open defiance in every sector of this alien province. It must be like watching vomit spew from the mouth of someone who's sick. How awful it must feel to be "despised and rejected by men" (Isaiah 53:3) and so completely misunderstood. Yet Jesus continues to be loving, kind, and patient.

As has been stated numerous times, much of the moral darkness in our world exists because earth's mixed-up masses don't understand God's heart. It was because of this lack of comprehension that Jesus Christ came to earth: He came to reveal God's heart. Ignoring unjust social mores, He welcomed outcasts, touched lepers, pardoned prostitutes, and ate with sinners. Compassion and love shone out from His every word, look, and act. He " 'did not come to destroy men's lives but to save them' " (Luke 9:56). He even washed the feet of His betrayer.

At the end of His earthly pilgrimage, Jesus performed the final act of supreme unselfishness: He drank that undiluted "cup" in Gethsemane and on Calvary. He died as an atoning sacrifice for the sins of every man, woman, and child who has ever lived, is now living, or ever shall live, and on a bright Sunday morning He rose from the dead. This is how God "demonstrates His own love toward us" (Romans 5:8). The loyal universe is fully convinced. None of Lucifer's seeds of doubt remain planted in their minds. Every holy angel knows that God is good.

Human beings who respond to this revelation, repent of their sins, trust in the blood of the Lamb, and rely firmly on the righteousness of Christ receive not only full forgiveness but also a new heart and heavenly power to live a new life. Revelation 14 describes a group of people who do just that. These end-time saints "keep the commandments of God and the faith of Jesus" (Revelation 14:12). They do it because they love Jesus.

Revelation 14 lists additional characteristics. Take a look.

> Then I looked, and behold, a Lamb standing on Mount Zion, and with Him one hundred and forty-four thousand, having His Father's name written on their foreheads. And I heard a voice from heaven, like the voice of many waters, and like the voice of

loud thunder. And I heard the sound of harpists playing their harps. They sang as it were a new song before the throne, before the four living creatures, and the elders; and no one could learn that song except the hundred and forty-four thousand who were redeemed from the earth. These are the ones who were not defiled with women, for they are virgins. These are the ones who follow the Lamb wherever He goes. These were redeemed from among men, being firstfruits to God and to the Lamb. And in their mouth was found no deceit, for they are without fault before the throne of God (Revelation 14:1–5).

This is an amazing prophecy. It describes the development of a special people during earth's last days called "the hundred and forty-four thousand." These people are portrayed as being with "the Lamb," as having "no deceit," and perhaps most significantly, as having the "Father's name written on their foreheads."

God's character within them

As we've seen, God's "name" is His true character, which takes us right back to Exodus 34:5–7. Revelation's message that this "name" will be "written" on the "foreheads" of the 144,000 must mean that *every aspect* of the divine character is to be incorporated into the thinking, perceptions, and emotions of these children of God. Don't miss the significance of this—prophecy predicts that the Lord's final people are to have His character "written" in their hearts and heads so that they themselves will reflect His goodness. Who do you think wants to stop this process? You know the answer. And how might he do it? It's easy to guess. By misrepresenting, distorting, and perverting the true character of God.

The battle is on inside our heads! It is no easy matter to detect Satan's imbalances and twisted maneuverings, and to discern what God is really like without falsification or distortion. And so a conflict occurs inside our hearts as we struggle to understand God's love and forgiveness and to trust in the fairness of His justice. Yes, the battle is on, and as we approach the end, the character of God controversy will only intensify.

The 144,000 will overcome. Standing with the Lamb on Mount Zion, they will have His Father's name written on their foreheads. Though the earth is "dark through misapprehension of God" (DA 22), and though millions view their Maker in "a false light" and "look upon Him as a ty-rant" (LHU 36), the 144,000 will cast their vote for the truth. "God is merciful and gracious," they will steadfastly affirm. "He is patient, and abundant in goodness and truth," they will tell the world. "He is forgiv-ing," they will teach by pen, voice, and acts. But there is another affirma-tion that will be indelibly "written" inside their heads: "God will by no means clear the guilty." The 144,000 will defend this too.

One of the most momentous truths taught in the Holy Bible, espe-cially in the book of Revelation, is that while mercy has flowed relent-lessly from a Father's tender heart for thousands of years, eventually, His justice will settle upon the guilty unmixed with mercy. Then humanity's appointed day of grace will cease. It will take much longer than sixty seconds to reach that point; but someday it will surely come. *This is what the Bible says.*

> God keeps a reckoning with the nations. Through every cen-tury of this world's history evil workers have been treasuring up wrath against the day of wrath; and when the time fully comes that iniquity shall have reached the stated boundary of God's mercy, *His forbearance will cease.* When the accumulated figures in heaven's record books shall mark the sum of transgression complete, *wrath will come, unmixed with mercy,* and then it will be seen what a tremendous thing it is to have worn out the divine patience. This crisis will be reached when the nations shall unite in making void God's law (5T 524; emphasis added).

A similar transition occurred in Noah's day. After Noah, his family, and the animals entered the ark, the boat's massive door miraculously closed, "and the LORD shut him in" (Genesis 7:16). That was it. Noah and his family were inside, while a world that had rejected God's message was outside. For seven days, the lost laughed. "Hey, Noah! Where's the water? Ha ha ha!" But on the seventh day, dark clouds gathered, "the windows of heaven were opened," the rain fell, and all life was "destroyed from the earth" (Genesis 7:11, 23).

" 'As the days of Noah were,' " Jesus plainly warned, " 'so also will the coming of the Son of Man be' " (Matthew 24:37). Just as the pre-Flood world was divided into two great groups—the saved and the lost—so shall it be at the end of time. Jesus Christ is now our High Priest in the sanctuary in heaven, ministering His own blood in behalf of fallen humankind (see Hebrews 8:1, 2; 9:12). Shortly before He returns, His ministry of grace will cease. Then will be made this solemn pronouncement: " 'He who is unjust, let him be unjust still; he who is filthy, let him be filthy still; he who is righteous, let him be righteous still; he who is holy, let him be holy still' " (Revelation 22:11).

When this time finally arrives, earth's doomed masses will be totally "unconscious that the final, irrevocable decision has been pronounced in the sanctuary above" (GC 491). They won't know that "every case has been decided for life or death" (GC 613). This won't be reported on CNN or on the nightly news, yet it will be so. The "decisive hour" will have come—"the final withdrawal of mercy's offer to guilty men" (GC 491). For the unsaved, it will be forever too late.

This solemn transition is described in Revelation 7 as the time when "four angels standing at the four corners of the earth" finally release "the four winds of the earth" (Revelation 7:1). These "winds" represent strife, war, bloodshed, natural disasters, the breaking out of human passion, and direct satanic fury. Whether we realize it or not, the Holy Spirit and holy angels are restraining these horrors at this very moment so that they don't completely overwhelm New York, Paris, Moscow, Mexico City, and every other city, town, and rural area in our world. Humanity's present problems are challenging, but much greater devastation is coming. Someday all four winds will be released, and then a " 'time of trouble, Such as never was since there was a nation' " (Daniel 12:1) will strike full force. It will be much worse than when Hurricane Katrina hit New Orleans.

The source of the final trouble

A large portion of this final "trouble" will come from Satan and his angels. By nature they are murderers and destroyers. Ever since the Fall, God has mercifully restrained their machinations. But when Jesus ceases His ministry in the sanctuary above,

> The restraint which has been upon the wicked is removed, and Satan has entire control of the finally impenitent. God's long-suffering has ended. The world has rejected His mercy, despised His love, and trampled upon His law. The wicked have passed the

boundary of their probation; the Spirit of God, persistently re-sisted, has been at last withdrawn. Unsheltered by divine grace, they have no protection from the wicked one. *Satan will then plunge the inhabitants of the earth into one great, final trouble.* As the angels of God cease to hold in check the fierce winds of hu-man passion, all the elements of strife will be let loose. The whole world will be involved in ruin more terrible than that which came upon Jerusalem of old (GC 614; emphasis added).

Back to the character of God controversy: many today interpret this final manifestation of Satan's wrath to be the complete definition of God's wrath. To them, God's wrath is nothing more than the devil's fury. In other words, once the four winds are released, Satan does every-thing while God does nothing—nothing, that is, but remove His re-straint from the wicked one.

To those who advocate this perspective, the very thought of God Himself directly causing any devastation is tantamount to making the Lord satanic too. "God would be a killer," they say in effect, "just like the fallen fiend!" And so, in their attempt to teach the truth about God, they blame sin and the devil for almost everything. Thus God's judgments described in Revelation are interpreted as merely the granting of apoca-lyptic permission—the giving of a final green light to an ancient foe to perform his dirty work, and nothing more.

As Martin Luther protested against many unbiblical religious tradi-tions, the authors of this book protest too. Luther wasn't looking for a fight, and neither are we. We also want Jesus' love in our hearts, just as those who sincerely teach the doctrine they propose. But honestly, we just don't believe it; and as with Luther, our consciences compel us. Yes, we know Satan is a murderer; and yes, we know that a large percentage of the global havoc during the time of trouble originates with him; nev-ertheless, we strongly disagree with the notion that Lucifer's fury is syn-onymous with God's wrath. And we especially disagree with the theory that God's directly punishing sin would make Him a sinister deity. Jesus not only called Satan a murderer but also a liar (see John 8:44). None of us wants to be deceived. So let's examine the evidence, and may the Lord help us all to discern His truth.

It's time we tackle Revelation 16, which is clearly the most graphically intense chapter in the entire Bible regarding the outpouring of divine wrath during the time of trouble. Revelation 15, which lays the groundwork, opens with this solemn scene: "I saw another sign in heaven, great and marvelous: seven angels having the seven last plagues, for in them the wrath of God is complete" (Revelation 15:1). This is the beginning of Revelation's message about the seven last plagues, also called "the wrath of God." These plagues are represented as being borne by "seven angels." That these angels are definitely God's angels and not Satan's angels is clear from the fact that they first appear *inside* the Lord's temple; they are "clothed in pure bright linen"; they obey God's instructions; and they descend from heaven (Revelation 15:6).

Now here's the first verse in Revelation chapter 16: "Then I heard a loud voice from the temple saying to the seven angels, 'Go and pour out the bowls of the wrath of God on the earth.' " Those who think the seven last plagues come from Satan and not from Jesus earnestly contend that it is vitally important that everyone understand their message. Their books, tapes, CDs, and Web sites teach this. But if this view is correct, then why is it that God doesn't seem to share this concern in Revelation 16 itself? If Jesus is so interested in having His people grasp the idea that it is Lucifer and his minions who actually implement the final plagues, then why does God's inspired Word state that they *come from God*?

"The reason," some might suggest, "is because God wants us to go deeper into the Scriptures to understand correct principles. Besides, all symbolism must be interpreted."

Our response is that we agree that all symbolism must be interpreted, that "winds" don't mean real gusts, etc., and that we should all study more deeply. Nevertheless we again inquire: if the seven last plagues don't really come from Jesus, and if this message is crucial for God's end-time saints to understand—if it's a "present truth"—*then why does Revelation 16 itself communicate the opposite message*? Is God playing mind games with us? We don't think so.

The seven plagues are as follows:

1. Boils afflict those who receive the mark of the beast (Revelation 16:2).
2. The ocean turns to blood (verse 3).
3. The rivers and fountains of water become blood (verse 4).

4. The sun scorches people with fire (verse 8).
5. Darkness falls upon the throne of the beast (verse 10).
6. The Euphrates River dries up (verse 12).
7. A great earthquake causes cities to crumble, mountains to sink, and islands to vanish, and then great hailstones fall (verses 17–21).

Consider these thoughts

It is not our purpose to analyze each plague thoroughly, but here are some thoughts to consider: In plague four, the sun scorches people with fire. Can Satan make the sun do this? Perhaps, but not likely. In plague five, darkness settles upon "the throne of the beast," which is really the devil's seat (see Revelation 12:9 and 13:2). Why would Lucifer bring darkness upon his own headquarters? In plague seven, the entire earth is devastated. This earth will be Satan's abode for a thousand years (see Revelation 19:17, 18; 20:1–3). Why would the devil depopulate the earth, initiate the millennium, and bring himself and his angelic comrades one step closer to the lake of fire and brimstone? This doesn't make sense. No, the Bible is clear. It is God—not Lucifer—"who has power over these plagues" (Revelation 16:9).

The key question is, If God does send these plagues, is He being just or unjust in doing so? Amazingly, Revelation 16 pictures two different groups who express two different perspectives, and it is important to realize *which* group expresses *which* perspective. First, let's notice the perspective of those who suffer the plagues. After the fourth plague, "they blasphemed the name of God who has power over these plagues; and they did not repent and give Him glory" (verse 9). After the fifth plague, "They blasphemed the God of heaven because of their pains and their sores, and did not repent of their deeds" (verse 11). During the seventh plague, "Men blasphemed God because of the plague of the hail, since that plague was exceedingly great" (verse 21).

Thus it is those on Satan's side of the great controversy who eventually blaspheme the name of God and God Himself because of these plagues. According to the verses quoted above, those people realize that it is "God who has power over these plagues," and they hate Him for it. What a solemn thought! May Jesus rescue us from this viewpoint, and keep us out of that camp.

Far different is the mind-set of those on the Lord's side. During the fourth plague, "the angel of the waters" declares,

"You are righteous, O Lord, . . .
Because You have judged these things.
For they have shed the blood of saints and prophets,
And You have given them blood to drink.
For it is their just due."

And I heard another from the altar, saying, "Even so, Lord God Almighty, *true and righteous are Your judgments*" (Revelation 16:5–7; emphasis added).

These inspired statements, rising from the heart of Revelation 16, reveal two key facts: (1) God is the Sender of these plagues, and (2) God is declared to be "true and righteous" in His actions. Thus, instead of "Satan did it!" being the message of Revelation 16, the inspired Word reveals that God sends the plagues, He is just in doing so, heavenly voices approve of His actions, and the lost blame Him and blaspheme His name. Notice this comment: "Terrible as these inflictions are, *God's justice stands fully vindicated.* The angel of God declares: 'Thou art righteous, O Lord, . . . because Thou hast judged thus. For they have shed the blood of saints and prophets, and Thou hast given them blood to drink; for they are worthy.' Revelation 16:2-6" (GC 628; emphasis added).

Additional light shines when we notice that these judgments are referred to as the seven *last* plagues (Revelation 15:1). The word *last* implies that all seven were preceded by earlier plagues of a similar character; and this is exactly the case. In the Old Testament, the Egyptians suffered under ten plagues, several of which resembled the seven last plagues. Both sets of plagues include sores (Exodus 9:9; Revelation 16:2), water turning to blood (Exodus 7:20; Revelation 16:3, 4), darkness (Exodus 10:22; Revelation 16:10), and hail (Exodus 9:23; Revelation 16:21).

So we inquire, who sent the ten plagues upon the Egyptians, God or Lucifer? The book of Exodus supplies a straightforward answer. " 'I will stretch out My hand,' " the Lord told Moses, " 'and strike Egypt with all My wonders which I will do in its midst' " (Exodus 3:20). Before each of the ten plagues, Moses and Aaron stood before Pharaoh to announce exactly what God was about to do. To start the first plague, the Lord told Aaron, " ' "Take your rod and stretch out your hand over the waters of Egypt, over their streams, over their rivers, over their ponds, and over all their pools of water, that they may become blood" ' " (Exodus 7:19). So Aaron obediently stretched out his rod and the waters of Egypt turned red.

Satan was active too, but not in sending the plagues. Instead, he produced subtle counterfeits through his servants, Pharaoh's magicians. After the first plague turned Egypt's water to blood, "the magicians of Egypt did so with their enchantments" (Exodus 7:22). And after the second plague of frogs, "the magicians . . . brought up frogs on the land of Egypt" (Exodus 8:7). But as the judgments advanced, the magicians' magical powers weakened. When nasty lice began crawling upon the Egyptians, "the magicians so worked with their enchantments to bring forth lice, but they could not. . . . Then the magicians said to Pharaoh, 'This is the finger of God' " (Exodus 8:18, 19).

So, God worked by sending the plagues, and Satan sought to counterfeit them. When the plagues fell upon the magic makers too (see Exodus 9:11), they finally realized that they had foolishly been fighting a superior power. "The magicians, the servants of Satan, at his command, tried to produce the same with their enchantments, but could not. The work of God was shown to be superior to the power of Satan. . . . When the magicians saw that they could not produce the lice, they said unto Pharaoh, 'This is the finger of God' " (1SP 187). They were 100 percent correct. God's finger, not Lucifer's, was causing those plagues.

The tenth plague

One, two, three, four, five, six, seven, eight, nine. Finally, the tenth plague was pending. " 'I will bring one more plague on Pharaoh and on Egypt,' " the Lord told Moses. " 'Afterward he will let you go' " (Exodus 11:1). Standing before the stubborn king one last time, "Moses said, 'Thus says the LORD: "About midnight I will go out into the midst of Egypt; and all the firstborn in the land of Egypt shall die" ' " (verses 4, 5).

The warning was horrific: *every firstborn child was to be slain, including Pharaoh's.* Nevertheless, as a revelation of God's character of love, a way of escape was offered to every Egyptian family, including that of the cruel monarch. The mark of protection would be the blood of a lamb.

Every father was urged to " ' "take for himself a lamb, according to the house of his father, a lamb for a household" ' " (Exodus 12:3). On a specified day, they were to " ' "kill it at twilight" ' " (verse 6). Then they were to " ' "take some of the blood and put it on the two doorposts and on the lintel of the houses" ' " where they lived (verse 7).

Why this strange ritual? The Lord Himself declared, " ' "I will pass through the land of Egypt on that night, and will strike all the firstborn in the land of Egypt, both man and beast; and against all the gods of Egypt I will execute judgment: I am the LORD. Now the blood shall be a sign for you on the houses where you are. And when I see the blood, I will pass over you; and the plague shall not be on you to destroy you when I strike the land of Egypt" ' " (Exodus 12:12, 13).

Those who obeyed the warning, slew the lamb, and smeared its blood on their doors were protected. Their children survived. But those who trusted their own heads, their own hearts, their own goodness, or their own gods suffered terrible consequences.

> At midnight "there was a great cry in Egypt: for there was not a house where there was not one dead." All the first-born in the land, "from the firstborn of Pharaoh that sat on his throne unto the firstborn of the captive that was in the dungeon; and all the firstborn of cattle" had been smitten by the destroyer. Through-out the vast realm of Egypt the pride of every household had been laid low. The shrieks and wails of the mourners filled the air. King and courtiers, with blanched faces and trembling limbs, stood aghast at the overmastering horror. Pharaoh remembered how he had once exclaimed, "Who is Jehovah, that I should obey His voice to let Israel go? I know not Jehovah, neither will I let Israel go." Now, his heaven-daring pride humbled in the dust, he "called for Moses and Aaron by night, and said, Rise up, and get you forth from among my people, both ye and the children of Israel; and go, serve the Lord, as ye have said." . . . The royal counselors also and the people entreated the Israelites to depart "out of the land in haste; for they said, We be all dead men" (PP 279, 280).

Even though the Bible says "the LORD struck all the firstborn" (Exodus 12:29), many suggest that it was really Satan who dealt the death-blow. To be fair, they have their reasons. From what I've read, the main reason—beyond their core belief that it is contrary to the character of God to directly punish sin—is that Exodus 12:23 states that it was "the destroyer" who did the job. Then they point to John 10:10, which says that it is Satan who comes " 'to kill, and to destroy,' " and to the fact that the book of Revelation gives the names *Abaddon* and *Apollyon,* which literally mean "a destroyer," to "the angel of the bottomless pit" (chapter 9:11). What about this?

First, there's no doubt that Satan is a destroyer. Second, it's also true that our loving Creator is by nature primarily a Life-Giver, not a life-taker. Nevertheless, it is one of the purposes of this book to demonstrate that, even though God "gives to all life, breath, and all things" (Acts 17:25), it is not contrary to His character to take life too, when He considers it necessary.

The plainest proof of this is the Lord's repeated commands to sinners—including the Israelites on Passover night—to slay lambs. No one, not even the most die-hard God-doesn't-kill advocate, can possibly deny that it was the Lord who issued these instructions. But just to clarify: God took " 'no pleasure' " in watching innocent animals die (Hebrews 10:6). Nevertheless, He did require those bloody rituals to teach us vivid lessons about the horror of sin and the future sacrifice of His Son. Thus our Creator can—and sometimes does—command the taking of life.

What about human life?

Let's return to the Word for the answer. Immediately after urging Christians to "contend earnestly for the faith," Jude stated that "the Lord, having *saved* the people out of the land of Egypt, afterward *destroyed* those who did not believe" (Jude 3, 5; emphasis added). Thus God both *saved* and *destroyed.* James agreed. "There is one Lawgiver," he wrote in his book, "who is able to save and to destroy" (James 4:12). If the Lord doesn't really destroy even though these verses say that He does, then what about salvation? Does He really save, or should this be reinterpreted too?

Who destroyed the firstborn in Egypt? The Bible states, "*The* LORD struck all the firstborn" (Exodus 12:29; emphasis added). Besides the Bible's statement, there are additional reasons why it couldn't have been Lucifer or one of his imps who destroyed them. Just think about it: the death of the firstborn was the final act that resulted in the deliverance of God's people. Why would Satan initiate that final act? Didn't he want to keep Israel in bondage? In fact, his activity through the magicians showed that he was fighting hard to keep Israel in Egypt, not to get them out of that land. Time after time God told Pharaoh, "Let My people go!" But the king kept refusing until finally the tenth plague convinced him. Why would Satan so obediently carry out God's will and bring the plague that resulted in Pharaoh releasing Israel?

No, Satan didn't slay the firstborn. His goal was to keep Israel in bondage. But God had other plans. And really, if Satan did do it, then he would be Israel's deliverer. But this can't be. Jude stated that it was "the Lord [who] . . . saved the people out of the land of Egypt" (Jude 5). Not only that, but he did so in a context of urging Christians to "contend earnestly" for these biblical facts against the subtle influence of false teachers (verse 3).

The blood of the Lamb

Moving beyond the identity of the death angel (whom we believe was definitely not a demon), there is something infinitely more important that must be stressed—the significance of the blood of the lamb. " ' "When I see the blood," ' " God Almighty told the Israelites, " ' "I will pass over you; and the plague shall not be on you to destroy you when I strike the land of Egypt" ' " (Exodus 12:13). Don't miss this. God considered the blood to be the key factor in whether the firstborn would survive or perish, and that blood represented the blood of His Son. Note carefully.

The only safety for the Israelites was blood upon the doorposts. God said, "When I see the blood, I will pass over you" (Ex. 12:13). All other devices for safety would be without avail. Nothing but the blood on the doorposts would bar the way that the angel of death should not enter. *There is salvation for the sinner in the blood of Jesus Christ alone, which cleanseth us from all sin.* The man with a cultivated intellect may have vast stores of knowledge, he may engage in theological speculations, he may be great and honored of men and be considered the repository of knowledge, but unless he has a saving knowledge of Christ crucified for him, and by faith lays hold of the righteousness of Christ, he is lost. Christ "was wounded for our transgressions, he was bruised for our iniquities: the chastisement of our peace was upon him; and with his stripes we are healed" (Isa. 53:5). *"Saved by the blood of Jesus Christ," will be our only hope for time and our song throughout eternity* (3 SM 172, 173; emphasis added).

Here lies the greatest message of the Passover ritual: the supreme importance of *the blood of the lamb.* It was by *blood* that the firstborn were spared the tenth plague. It was by *blood* that God's people were freed from Egyptian slavery. It was by *blood* that Israel became a nation. And if the soon coming seven last plagues parallel the ancient ten plagues, which they do, then what must be one of Heaven's most urgent messages to prepare us for those awesome days? *It must be the importance of the blood of the Lamb.*

The book of Romans connects faith in the blood of Jesus Christ, which has been made available by God's *mercy,* with being delivered from "the wrath to come" (1 Thessalonians 1:10), which is a manifestation of His *justice.* Take a look: "God demonstrates His own love toward us, in that while we were still sinners, Christ died for us. Much more then, having now been *justified by His blood,* we shall be *saved from wrath* through Him" (Romans 5:8, 9).

Paul says that if we are justified by Jesus' blood, then we need not fear *His wrath.* Conversely, if we reject that blood, especially at the end of time, then when mercy ceases and the seven last plagues start falling, we will have no protection. And just as was true in Egypt, we must personally apply that blood to our own lives and to that of our families. Only in this will we find safety.

Just before the firstborn were slain in Egypt, the Lord instructed the Israelites to gather their children into their houses with them, and to strike the lintel and the two side posts of their doors with blood, so that when the destroying angel went through the land, he would recognize the houses thus marked as the dwelling places of Christ's followers, and pass over them.

Today we must gather our children about us if we desire to save them from the destructive power of the evil one. The conflict between Christ and Satan will increase in intensity until the end of this earth's history. *We are to have faith in the blood of Christ in order that we may pass safely through the perilous times just before us* (2 SAT 199).

There is yet another vital lesson in Revelation 16. Sandwiched between the sixth and seventh plagues lies one oft-overlooked verse spoken directly by Jesus Christ to His end-time people immediately prior to the battle of Armageddon. Here is it: " 'Behold, I am coming as a thief. Blessed is he who watches, and keeps his garments, lest he walk naked and they see his shame' " (verse 15).

Here the returning King identifies both the wearing and keeping of "garments" as the key to not walking "naked" when the plagues hit. Other verses in the Apocalypse shed light on what these garments represent. Speaking to the church of Sardis, Jesus Christ urged His hearers to be " 'clothed in white garments' " (Revelation 3:1–5). In His message to the church of the Laodiceans, He told His people to put on " 'white garments, that you may be clothed, that the shame of your nakedness may not be revealed' " (Revelation 3:14, 18). And finally, as John gazed beyond this dark world to heaven's glory, he beheld a victorious group "clothed with white robes . . . crying out with a loud voice, saying, 'Salvation belongs to our God who sits on the throne, and to the Lamb!' " (Revelation 7:9, 10) The garments that Jesus urges His people to keep throughout the time of the seven plagues are the white garments of His own perfect righteousness, which, as we saw earlier, He now offers to impute and impart to us *in place* of our sins.

So, at the same time that Revelation 16 warns us about the final outpouring of the wrath of God unmixed with mercy, it also offers supreme security through trusting the blood of the Lamb and being clothed in His righteousness. As in the days of ancient Egypt, the Lord's comforting promise to each of us before earth's final crisis is, " ' "When I see the blood, I will pass over you; and the plague shall not be on you to destroy you when I strike the land of Egypt" ' " (Exodus 12:13).

The purpose of the plagues

As we near the end of this chapter, there is something else we must contemplate that not only demonstrates God's intense love for His people but also sheds light on exactly *why* He chooses to pour out the seven plagues in the first place. Think hard about this: *why* did Jesus send ten plagues upon Pharaoh and the Egyptians?

"To free Israel from slavery," you may say.

Yes, but from what sort of slavery? Was Egypt like most United States correction facilities that treat their inmates humanely?

Hardly. The Pharaoh who came to the throne after the time of Joseph was unbelievably cruel. Not only did he set taskmasters over the Israelites to make "their lives bitter with hard bondage" (Exodus 1:11, 14), but he also went after their kids. That Pharaoh commanded his soldiers that whenever a Hebrew boy was born, they were either to kill the child immediately or to cast it into the Nile River to drown or to be devoured by crocodiles (verses 16, 22). These are only some of the reasons why the Israelites "groaned because of their bondage" and "cried out" to God (Exodus 2:23). Behind the scenes, Satan and his demons were working to wipe out God's people entirely. But before they could do so, God sent Moses, Aaron, and the plagues.

The end time will be similar. When the four angels release the four winds, Satan will not only have "entire control of the finally impenitent" (GC 614), but he will then fire up those who have chosen to serve him with hellish inspiration "to destroy God's people in the time of trouble" (ibid., 618). As this totally loveless, eerie movement of death gathers momentum after the close of human probation (see Revelation 22:11), Jesus will no longer seek to save its devil-possessed participants, but only to protect and defend His church, the apple of His eye.

As Satan's global conglomerate beholds God's helpless remnant of fathers, mothers, husbands, wives, children, orphans, widows, and single believers fleeing to the mountains, huddling together in small companies, supporting each other, and praying for each other, its doomed members will be satanically charged with one primary, primal emotion. That emotion will be *hate*—a sinister, uncontrollable hatred for both God and His people. Jesus saw it coming. He knew what human beings would degenerate into when the Holy Spirit fully withdrew from them. That's why He forewarned His followers, saying, " 'You will be hated by all for My name's sake' " (Luke 21:17). Such is the ugly nature of sin. The situation was bad in Egypt, but it will be much worse during the time of trouble.

Have you heard the popular question, "What would Jesus do?" Well, what *will* our Savior do when the entire world unites to butcher His church and the blood of the martyrs cries out for vengeance (see Revelation 6:10, 11)? Obviously, by that time He will have already given up the wicked to their fearful course; but is that it? The "Revelation of Jesus Christ" (Revelation 1:1) reveals the answer. After thousands of years of mercy, it's time for a change. As Satan's evil army stealthily advances for the kill, Jesus Christ will act—not now as heaven's Lamb, but as " 'the Lion of the tribe of Judah' " to express "the fierceness and wrath of Almighty God" (Revelation 5:5; 19:15).

"The cruelty done to God's servants is recorded as done to Christ in the person of His saints, *and the time is coming when God Himself will avenge their wrongs"* (ST, March 28, 1900; emphasis added). Seated on His royal throne beyond the stars, King Jesus will then command His angels, " 'Go and pour out the bowls of the wrath of God on the earth' " (Revelation 16:1). Then the seven last plagues, "the most awful scourges that have ever been known to mortals," will fall "unmixed with mercy" (GC 628, 629).

When those fearful judgments hit, as terrible as they are, "the angel of the waters" will nevertheless affirm, " 'You are righteous O Lord, . . . Because You have judged these things' " (Revelation 16:5). And as the entire universe watches closely every move the Almighty makes, its verdict will be crystal clear: "God's justice stands fully vindicated" (GC 628).

As we close this chapter, let's address one more highly practical issue. "All this sounds scary!" I hear someone say, "I hope I don't have to endure the time of trouble!"

I won't lie. Yes, it will be scary. But the good news is that if we repent of our sins and maintain childlike trust in Jesus Christ's blood and in the power of His righteousness, we will be fully secure. Our Savior's eye will be upon us, and He won't look away for one minute. "The arm strong to smite the rebellious will be strong to deliver the loyal" (AA 589).

Read and memorize Psalm 91. Among its greatest assurances are these lines:

> He who dwells in the secret place of the Most High
> Shall abide under the shadow of the Almighty . . .
> No evil shall befall you,
> Nor shall any plague come near your dwelling;
> For He shall give His angels charge over you,

To keep you in all your ways (verses 1, 10, 11).

Praise God when the enemy closes in, the company of guardian angels stationed around God's people will double. Read the entire chapter titled "The Time of Trouble" in Ellen G. White's book *The Great Controversy*. While we don't know exactly how long that time of trouble will last, it won't be too long, and its end will bring the dawning of the eternal day. As the famous Christian hymn says, "There'll be no dark valley when Jesus comes to carry His loved ones home."

A little girl became frightened one night while lying alone in her bed. Running into her parents' bedroom, she pleaded, "Daddy, can I sleep with you tonight? I'm scared!"

"Sure, honey," came the loving response, "climb in."

But after a few minutes of lying in pitch darkness near her father, the child was still afraid. "Daddy," she called out again, "is your face toward me?"

"Yes, little one," her dad replied, snuggling closer, "my face is toward you."

Comforted, the girl fell asleep.

We can have the same comfort. No matter what happens, Jesus has promised, " 'Lo, I am with you always, even to the end of the age' " (Matthew 28:20). And Peter counseled us to cast "all your care upon Him, for He cares for you" (1 Peter 5:7).

When the population of the entire universe is reckoned in the count, there are far more who love God than who don't, and far more good angels than devils. More importantly, the Lord is much stronger than Satan, so we don't need to be afraid. And not only is Jesus Christ our loving Savior, but He is also our best Friend, Protector, Defender, and Deliverer. Evil doesn't have a chance. Soon King Jesus will crush Lucifer and take us home.

For Further Thought and Discussion

1. Read Revelation 14:1. The Bible says that God's end-time people—the 144,000—will have His name written on their foreheads. What does this mean?
2. What will God's end-time people be like?
3. In what ways might Satan be working to prevent them from becoming what God wants them to be?
4. Why will mercy cease?
5. When mercy ceases, what will Satan do to his own people?
6. When mercy ceases, what will Satan do—or try to do—to God's people?
7. When mercy ceases, what will God do to Satan's people, and why?
8. When mercy ceases, what will God do for His own people?
9. What can we do now to prepare for the time of trouble?
10. What impressed you the most in this chapter, and why?

CHAPTER 9

THE END OF EVIL

In everything one must consider the end.

—Jean de La Fontaine

"One far-off, divine event to which the whole creation moves." This inspiring sentence from Alfred Lord Tennyson appears on one of the walls inside the Library of Congress in Washington, D.C. For more than one hundred years, people have pondered the meaning of this famous sentence. Tour guides still draw attention to it. Presidents, legislators, and politicians still consider it.

This "far-off, divine event" most likely refers to the day of judgment. Students of prophecy, especially of the book of Revelation, understand that this unique event occurs at the close of the millennium. At the second coming of Jesus Christ, which takes place at the beginning of the millennium, the redeemed of all ages rise from their dusty graves in " 'the resurrection of life' " (John 5:29; see also 1 Thessalonians 4:16, 17). This is "the first resurrection," the resurrection of the "blessed" (Revelation 20:6). At the end of the millennium, a vastly different awakening occurs. Jesus called this latter, or second, resurrection, " 'the resurrection of condemnation' " (John 5:29; see Revelation 20:5). In one terribly solemn panoramic sweep, John describes the close of the millennium, this second resurrection, the day of judgment, and the doom of the lost:

> The rest of the dead did not live again until the thousand years were finished. . . .
>
> Now when the thousand years have expired, Satan will be released from his prison. . . .

Then I saw a great white throne and Him who sat on it, from whose face the earth and the heaven fled away. And there was found no place for them. And I saw the dead, small and great, standing before God, and books were opened. And another book was opened, which is the Book of Life. And the dead were judged according to their works, by the things which were written in the books. The sea gave up the dead who were in it, and Death and Hades delivered up the dead who were in them. And they were judged, each one according to his works. Then Death and Hades were cast into the lake of fire. This is the second death. And anyone not found written in the Book of Life was cast into the lake of fire (Revelation 20:5, 7, 11–15).

These momentous events should grip us all. They are infinitely more significant than the highly publicized antics of Britney Spears or Madonna, or who wins the Super Bowl, or even what happens inside the White House. Our purpose in focusing on them is two-fold: (1) to stress the importance of being on God's side in the great war, and (2) to discover what these events reveal about His character. We must analyze closely the resurrection of the lost, the day of judgment, and the final destruction of the lost in the lake of fire. Much is at stake.

The resurrection of the lost

First, let's look at the resurrection of the lost. John wrote, "I saw the dead, small and great, standing before God" (Revelation 20:12). The fact that there even is a second resurrection is deeply significant. The question should be asked, why bring them out of their graves at all? Why not just leave them buried forever?

The most logical answer is that justice requires something more. These people have committed serious sins during their sojourn on earth, and they must be held accountable for these sins. Another reason is that God must value so highly the individuality, reasoning, and consciences of all of His creatures—including the lost—that He wants everyone to fully understand exactly *why* the lost are excluded from His kingdom. Before the entire universe, including before the wicked, righteousness must be exalted, truth revealed, and sin exposed. God must be revealed as perfectly

innocent, marvelously merciful, and supremely loving in all of His dealings with human beings and devils.

What an incredible moment when bones reconnect with bones and
"the dead, small and great," suddenly find themselves "standing before
God" (Revelation 20:12)! And we're not talking about just a few lost
souls. Instead, their "number is as the sand of the sea" (verse 8). It's im-
possible to do the math fully, but there may well be scores of billions of
people! All the lost who have ever lived—from the days of Adam to the
second coming of Jesus Christ—come forth, a mighty host. Of course,
none of them were anticipating this event before they died. Some believed in reincarnation, some expected to enter the spirit world, others
assumed that at death they would instantly soar through the pearly gates,
and still others believed they would rest in peace forever and that's it—
nothing more, just oblivion. But they were all wrong, dead wrong. The
time for truth has come.

> They come forth, a mighty host, numberless as the sands of
> the sea. What a contrast to those who were raised at the first res-
> urrection! The righteous were clothed with immortal youth and
> beauty. The wicked bear the traces of disease and death. . . .
>   . . . As the wicked went into their graves, so they come forth
> with the same enmity to Christ and the same spirit of rebellion.
> They are to have no new probation in which to remedy the de-
> fects of their past lives. Nothing would be gained by this. A life-
> time of transgression has not softened their hearts. A second pro-
> bation, were it given them, would be occupied as was the first in
> evading the requirements of God and exciting rebellion against
> him (GC 662).

Revelation 20 is clear that one of the primary reasons why the lost are
resurrected at the close of the millennium is so that they can be judged.
This is stated in verse 12 and repeated in verse 13. The Bible also says that
the lost are to be judged "each one according to his works" "by the things
which were written in the books" (Revelation 20:12, 13). This implies
that *all* their works, both good and bad, have been recorded, and that
nothing has been lost. In the judgment, everything will be taken into
consideration.

As soon as the books of record are opened, and the eye of Jesus looks upon the wicked, they are conscious of every sin which they have ever committed. They see just where their feet diverged from the path of purity and holiness, just how far pride and rebellion have carried them in the violation of the law of God. The seductive temptations which they encouraged by indulgence in sin, the blessings perverted, the messengers of God despised, the warnings rejected, the waves of mercy beaten back by the stubborn, unrepentant heart—all appear as if written in letters of fire (GC 666).

"Their works follow them"

As we found previously, a person's works mean more than mere actions, and much more is involved than just the internal effects of such acts upon the actor. The judgement must consider people's influence, which continues long after their funeral services. Speaking of the dead, the Word says that " 'their works follow them' " (Revelation 14:13). Joanne Kathleen Rowling has written seven Harry Potter books, the effects of which will continue until Jesus comes. The same is true of Oprah Winfrey's life, and of the life of every other person, great or small. This is why "the influence exerted for good or for evil, with its far-reaching results" is also "chronicled by the recording angel" (GC 482).

The implications of this are vital. In the character of God controversy, some conclude that the only penalty of sin is its internal effect upon the sinner. So, in contemplating the second resurrection, they believe that the only consequences that the lost will reap at the close of the millennium will be natural ones. They imagine that after the judgment, the penalty of sin will be somewhat comparable to allowing a smoker to develop lung cancer and die. While there is some truth here, for there are indeed personal consequences to sin, much more is involved.

Consider this: What if Joe Smoker also seduced nineteen teenagers to take up the habit? Is there no accountability for this too? Or what about the drug dealer who hooked twenty-five kids on crack, which resulted in twelve suicides? Or what about the publishers of *Playboy* and *Hustler* magazines, which have contributed to the ruin of many marriages? Praise God, forgiveness is available for every sin—but what will happen to those who not only despised His love and mercy but also led many others astray?

As innumerable resurrected lost souls sway like drunks before the pristine purity of God's great white throne, they will realize for the first time that no sin they ever committed has been forgotten, and neither have the far-reaching results. When these people are "judged, each one according to his works," they will be held to strict accountability. Why? Because the royal Judge is totally honest, completely impartial, and infinitely fair. His justice requires it.

At the end of the millennium, as billions of dead people suddenly awake to review their life history based on what has been written in the books, God will also reveal to each participant through some sort of panoramic video clip just how much He loved them and how hard He worked to prevent them from ending up outside the New Jerusalem. Only then will they discover the full magnitude of the mercy they so foolishly despised!

Above the throne is revealed the cross; and like a panoramic view appear the scenes of Adam's temptation and fall, and the successive steps in the great plan of redemption. The Saviour's lowly birth; His early life of simplicity and obedience; His baptism in Jordan; the fast and temptation in the wilderness; His public ministry, unfolding to men heaven's most precious blessings; the days crowded with deeds of love and mercy, the nights of prayer and watching in the solitude of the mountains; the plottings of envy, hate, and malice which repaid His benefits; the awful, mysterious agony in Gethsemane beneath the crushing weight of the sins of the whole world; His betrayal into the hands of the murderous mob; the fearful events of that night of horror—the unresisting prisoner, forsaken by His best-loved disciples, rudely hurried through the streets of Jerusalem; the Son of God exultingly displayed before Annas, arraigned in the high priest's palace, in the judgment hall of Pilate, before the cowardly and cruel Herod, mocked, insulted, tortured, and condemned to die—all are vividly portrayed.

And now before the swaying multitude are revealed the final scenes—the patient Sufferer treading the path to Calvary; the Prince of heaven hanging upon the cross; the haughty priests and the jeering rabble deriding His expiring agony; the supernatural darkness; the heaving earth, the rent rocks, the open graves, marking the moment when the world's Redeemer yielded up His life.

The awful spectacle appears just as it was. Satan, his angels, and his subjects have no power to turn from the picture of their own work. Each actor recalls the part which he performed. Herod, who slew the innocent children of Bethlehem that he might destroy the King of Israel; the base Herodias, upon whose guilty soul rests the blood of John the Baptist; the weak, timeserving Pilate; the mocking soldiers; the priests and rulers and the maddened throng who cried, "His blood be on us, and our children!"—all behold the enormity of their guilt. They vainly seek to hide from the divine majesty of His countenance, outshining the glory of the sun, while the redeemed cast their crowns at the Saviour's feet, exclaiming: "He died for me!" (GC 666, 667).

This will be one of the most awesome moments of all time. Everyone who has ever lived will be present—all together and alive at the same time! Peering breathlessly through the New Jerusalem's shiny walls will be the redeemed of all ages, while outside stand Satan, his angelic companions in crime, and every human being who has been incorrigibly duped by their deceptive schemes. In addition to these, above the earth will be the onlooking hosts of holy angels and the loyal inhabitants of other worlds (see Job 1:6). Unnumbered eyes will be watching anxiously as each momentous, never to be repeated event unfolds. And in the midst of all will be Jesus Christ Himself, the great center of cosmic attention, still bearing the marks of His love on His hands and feet, seated majestically upon His throne.

Love they have ignored

As the doomed and the damned gaze upon their Creator—the Gethsemane Man and Crucified One—surely they will sense His love and realize what they chose to ignore! "A flash of light will come to all lost souls" (UL 203). In that unique, revelatory moment, the entire body of unsaved sinners—human and angelic—will realize that their Maker is not to blame for the existence of sin or for its continuation or for its consequences. The Lord will stand innocent, fully exonerated by His entire universe of all guilt in the great controversy. Even the prince of darkness will acknowledge God's goodness. Then this Scripture will be fulfilled: "that at the name of Jesus every knee should bow, of those in heaven, and of those on earth, and of those under the earth, and that every tongue should confess that Jesus Christ is Lord, to the glory of God the Father" (Philippians 2:10, 11).

"Satan sees that his voluntary rebellion has unfitted him for heaven. He has trained his powers to war against God; the purity, peace, and harmony of heaven would be to him supreme torture. His accusations against the mercy and justice of God are now silenced. The reproach which he has endeavored to cast upon Jehovah rests wholly upon himself. And now Satan bows down and confesses the justice of his sentence" (GC 670).

Finally, the awful moment will come, the moment of sentence and then retribution.

> In the presence of the assembled inhabitants of earth and heaven the final coronation of the Son of God takes place. And now, invested with supreme majesty and power, the King of kings pronounces sentence upon the rebels against His government, and executes justice upon those who have transgressed His law and oppressed His people (GC 666).

> The whole wicked world stand arraigned at the bar of God, on the charge of high treason against the government of heaven. They have none to plead their cause; they are without excuse; and the sentence of eternal death is pronounced against them (GC 668).

It's time to closely consider this "sentence of eternal death" pronounced by King Jesus "upon the rebels against His government." Concerning this same sentence, Paul declared, "The wages of sin is death" (Romans 6:23). The Greek word translated "wages" is *opsonion*. The same word is used in Luke 3:14, which depicts John the Baptist urging Roman soldiers to " 'be content with your wages.' " *The New Strong's Dictionary of Hebrew and Greek Words* defines *opsonion*, or "wages," as "*rations* for a soldier, . . . his *stipend* or *pay*:—wages."[1]

The big question is *who pays* these wages at the end of the millennium? Some think that sin itself exacts the final wages, but the Bible doesn't teach this. It is true that in this life sin does carry frightful consequences and that the verse "Evil shall slay the wicked" (Psalm 34:21) is often fulfilled. Yet the Bible never applies such consequences to the final retribution after the great white throne judgment. Can sin be trusted to deal impartially? Borrowing a phrase from Fox News Channel, would it be "fair and balanced"? Hardly.

The Bible affirms, " 'Vengeance is Mine, *I will repay*,' says the Lord" (Hebrews 10:30; emphasis added). This is precisely what Jesus Christ taught. " 'The Son of Man will come in the glory of His Father with His angels, and then *He will reward* each according to his works' " (Matthew 16:27; emphasis added). Again, King Jesus declared, " '*I will give* to each one of you according to your works' " (Revelation 2:23; emphasis added). These verses indicate that it is God, not sin, who will administer the final retribution.

It must be so. In Romans 6:23—the "wages of sin" text—the Greek word translated "sin" is *hamartia,* which means "breaking the law," or "lawlessness." (See also 1 John 3:4, where the same word is used.) As we saw earlier, sin has to do with the Ten Commandments, and it applies to specific things like idolatry (second commandment), irreverence (third commandment), Sabbath breaking (fourth commandment), disrespect for parents (fifth commandment), and covetousness (tenth commandment). Above all, it is failing to love God and our neighbor as ourselves (see Matthew 22:34–40). The truth is that sin isn't smart enough to justly calculate the appropriate "wages" for each of these violations, especially when "the influence exerted for good or for evil, with its far-reaching results" is carefully considered. In fact, sin is supremely stupid. The following quote makes the truth plain: "*God has given in His word decisive evidence that He will punish the transgressors of His law.* Those who flatter themselves that He is too merciful to execute justice upon the sinner, have only to look to the cross of Calvary. The death of the spotless Son of God testifies that 'the wages of sin is death,' that every violation of God's law must receive its just retribution" (GC 539, 540; emphasis added).

It is God who will "punish the transgressors of His law" and administer "the wages of sin," just as it was God who executed justice on Calvary. According to the above quotation, He has given "decisive evidence" for this "in His word." We have just seen the evidence in Hebrews 10:30, Matthew 16:27, and Revelation 2:23, and these verses don't need to be reinterpreted. No, "God means just what He says" (HP 32).

Here's another key statement: "If [people today] refuse the heavenly benefit and choose the pleasures and deceitfulness of sin, they have their choice, and at the end receive *their wages, which is the wrath of God and eternal death.* They will be forever separated from the presence of Jesus, whose sacrifice they had despised" (2T 210; emphasis added).

Judged according to their works

As we've already seen, the Bible says that before the lost receive this retribution, they will be judged "each one according to his works" (Revelation 20:13). People's works vary, so it's logical to conclude that the payments will vary too. Surely a teenager who spurned Jesus' love should be treated differently than Saddam Hussein, who murdered multiple thousands. And surely the man who cheated on his wife and refused to repent will not reap the same reward as Nazi leaders who instigated the Holocaust. What earthly judge would pronounce the same sentence upon a shoplifter as upon a serial killer? Not one.

Abraham once inquired of God rhetorically, " 'Shall not the Judge of all the earth do right?' " (Genesis 18:25). No doubt He will. So, because people's sins and works vary, their resulting "wages" must vary too. Jesus Christ—who revealed God's character perfectly—clearly taught this when He said, " 'That servant who knew his master's will, and did not prepare himself or do according to his will, shall be beaten with many stripes. But he who did not know, yet committed things deserving of stripes, shall be beaten with few' " (Luke 12:47, 48).

This differentiation is only fair. And remember, at the close of the millennium, the whole universe will be closely monitoring God's actions. Innumerable lost humans whose offenses were comparatively minor, such as the socialite housewife who merely considered Christianity distasteful, will have to stand before the righteous Judge. And on the opposite end of the spectrum will be gang leaders, Mafia members, serial killers, child abusers, al-Qaida masterminds, and Lucifer himself—the worst of them all. Surely this situation requires the Just One to personally take matters into His own hands and to distribute fair wages. He *alone* can do it responsibly; and He will. His justice requires this.

Every question of truth and error in the long-standing controversy has now been made plain. The results of rebellion, the fruits of setting aside the divine statutes, have been laid open to the view of all created intelligences. The working out of Satan's rule in contrast with the government of God has been presented to the whole universe. Satan's own works have condemned him. *God's wisdom, His justice, and His goodness stand fully vindicated.* It is seen that all His dealings in the great controversy have been conducted with respect to the eternal good of His people and the good of all the worlds that He has created. "All thy works shall praise Thee, O Lord; and Thy saints shall bless Thee." Psalm 145:10. The history of sin will stand to all eternity as a witness that with the existence of God's law is bound up the happiness of all the beings He has created. *With all the facts of the great controversy in view, the whole universe, both loyal and rebellious, with one accord declare: "Just and true are Thy ways, Thou King of saints"* (GC 670, 671; emphasis added).

Then it will happen. After the judgment, "fire came down *from God* out of heaven and devoured them" (Revelation 20:9; emphasis added). Notice that the final retribution comes "from God," not from sin, sinners, or Satan. As to the specific details of this punishment, we won't speculate, for this hasn't been revealed. But based on Revelation 20:9, we know that fire will play a role in the destruction of the wicked. We also know that the Bible also compares God's presence to fire. "Our God is a consuming fire," wrote Paul (Hebrews 12:29). Read the following paragraph carefully.

[God's destruction of the wicked] *is not an act of arbitrary power on the part of God.* The rejecters of His mercy reap that which they have sown. God is the fountain of life; and when one chooses the service of sin, he separates from God, and thus cuts himself off from life. He is "alienated from the life of God." Christ says, "All they that hate Me love death." Eph. 4:18; Prov. 8:36. God gives them existence for a time that they may develop their character and reveal their principles. This accomplished, they receive the results of their own choice. By a life of rebellion, Satan and all who unite with him place themselves so out of harmony with God that *His very presence is to them a consuming fire. The glory of Him who is love will destroy them* (DA 764; emphasis added).

God-doesn't-kill advocates often quote this paragraph to support their viewpoint. "See," they contend, "the destruction of the wicked isn't 'arbitrary.' The lost cut themselves off from life and reap what they have sown. God doesn't do it; sin does!"

What does "arbitrary" mean? Many assume it means anything beyond natural consequences, but this isn't true. *Merriam-Webster's Online Dictionary* includes such concepts as "the unrestrained and often tyrannical exercise of power," "determined by individual preference or convenience," and "coming about seemingly at random or by chance or as a capricious and unreasonable act of will" in its definition of *arbitrary*.[2] Based on these definitions, none of God's actions—including His destruction of the wicked—are arbitrary. Everything He does is based on righteousness, justice, and above all, intelligent love. He isn't "tyrannical," "capricious," or "unreasonable."

Also, I urge you to take a closer look at the last part of the above quotation: "the glory of Him who is love will destroy them." What "destroy[s] them"? God's glory. What is His glory? You know the answer. It is God's character (see Exodus 33:18–21; 34:5–7). Thus it is God Himself who destroys them in accordance with *who He really is*—as it is written:

> The LORD preserves all who love Him,
> But all the wicked *He will destroy* (Psalm 145:20; emphasis added).

Like what Jesus experienced

This final, dreadful retribution will be in some sense similar to what Jesus experienced on the cross. Scripture says, "Christ died for our sins" (1 Corinthians 15:3). Christ's death was not a normal death, like the death people die today. It was a different kind of death. On Calvary He experienced the full "wages of sin" (Romans 6:23), which ends in "the second death" (Revelation 20:14). So far, no one has ever died that death but Jesus. Because of His great sacrifice, if we repent of our sins and trust Him fully, we're clear—we will never have to taste that retribution, thank God! But those who resist Christ's love and refuse His salvation will taste that death. They will experience it at the close of the millennium. "Those who reject the mercy so freely proffered, will yet be made to know the worth of that which they have despised. *They will feel the agony which Christ endured upon the cross to purchase redemption for all who would receive it.* And they will then realize what they have lost,—eternal life and the immortal inheritance" (RH, Sept. 4, 1883; emphasis added).

How tragic! What the lost finally suffer was completely avoidable. As the famous hymn says, "Jesus paid it all." But because the lost rejected Jesus' love and mercy and His endurance in their place of the wages of their sins, they must suffer that punishment themselves, and they can't survive it. "Some are destroyed as in a moment, while others suffer many days. All are punished 'according to their deeds' " (GC 673). "They suffer punishment varying in duration and intensity, 'according to their works,' but finally ending in the second death. . . . Covered with infamy, they sink into hopeless, eternal oblivion" (GC 544, 545).

What about the prince of evil himself, the worst offender of all? As can be expected, "his punishment is to be far greater than that of those whom he has deceived. After all have perished who fell by his deceptions, he is still to live and suffer on" (GC 673).

Again, this is only fair. Satan is the root instigator of all sin, lies, suffering, and pain. He is Jesus Christ's personal enemy, and he will be punished by Jesus Himself and then blotted out of existence. " '*I destroyed you, O covering cherub*' " (Ezekiel 28:16; emphasis added), Christ predicted in the Old Testament. The New Testament affirms that because of Jesus Christ's incarnation and death, "*He [will] destroy him who [has] the power of death, that is, the devil*" (Hebrews 2:14; emphasis added). Again, the exact details of this destruction have not been revealed. The important thing to know is that *God* does it, and that He will be entirely fair and just as He does it.

Many people have asked why Jesus didn't eliminate Satan at the very outset of the great war, when he first rebelled in heaven. Wouldn't this have prevented a lot of problems?

Yes and no. Yes, it might have prevented human sin, but the artful questions Satan had raised about the Lord's goodness would have remained in other angel hearts like hard to detect cancer cells capable of becoming malignant at any moment. Lucifer held high responsibilities in God's government, and then he rebelled. If he had simply vanished one day before any concrete evidence had surfaced against him, some of his angel friends might have thought that perhaps he had a point. God, whose perspective is infinite, realized this. In His far-reaching wisdom, He knew that Lucifer must be given the time necessary to prove that he was really a devil. And so, God patiently granted His enemy enough rope to hang himself.

"When [Lucifer] sinned in heaven, even the loyal angels did not fully discern his character. *This was why God did not at once destroy Satan.* Had He done so, the holy angels would not have perceived the justice and love of God. A doubt of God's goodness would have been as evil seed that would yield the bitter fruit of sin and woe. *Therefore the author of evil was spared, fully to develop his character*" (COL 72; emphasis added).

Don't miss this. The reason God didn't destroy Satan at once was *not* because such an act would have been contrary to His principles. Instead, it was because He is much too smart. He knew that such an act wouldn't make His universe eternally secure. The timing was wrong. It is at the close of the millennium, after sin has fully run its course, that all the inhabitants of the universe will fully and clearly discern the evil character of Satan, the justice and love of God, and His reasons for ending Satan's life. Then, "the power and authority of the divine government will be employed to put down rebellion; yet all the manifestations of retributive justice will be perfectly consistent with the character of God as a merciful, long-suffering, benevolent being" (GC 541).

Worse than an earthly parent?

Despite all the evidence presented in this book, some may still say, "Wait a minute! Even the lost are still God's children. Earthly parents love their kids no matter what they do. No loving father would ever deliberately terminate his son's life, so how can God do it?"

This is a fair question, and there's a good answer. Imagine a father who had three sons, and one of them went bad. Would he still love the wayward boy? Yes. But what if the evil son not only hurt himself by revolting against his father but also deliberately plotted to destroy his two brothers and even the father himself? Under such circumstances, would the father be justified in using force to stop his own offspring? We think so. What father wouldn't use force if his family were threatened?

Now let's go a step further. Let's say the evil son was successful in brutally killing his two brothers and his dad, but then he was arrested. Would we accuse the judge of injustice if he sentenced him to death row? And how about the man who administered the lethal injection? Would we consider him a murderer or even a torturer? Few would. Even in our secular society, the majority would fully support this decision and action. The police, the judge, and even the executioner are our protectors, not our enemies. That's true of Jesus Christ too. He is our eternal Protector and Defender. The ugly nature of sin is such that it eventually becomes a sinister, calculating threat to everything good. Sin would destroy us all if left unchecked, and it would even kill God. The Heart Searcher understands this perfectly, and so, for the good of His entire universe, at the end of the millennium, He will eliminate evil personally, directly, entirely, and permanently. The following paragraphs picture this perfectly.

God's love is represented in our day as being of such a character as would forbid His destroying the sinner. Men reason from their own low standard of right and justice. "Thou thoughtest that I was altogether such an one as thyself" (Ps. 50:21). They measure God by themselves. They reason as to how they would act under the circumstances and decide God would do as they imagine they would do. . . .

In no kingdom or government is it left to the lawbreakers to say what punishment is to be executed against those who have broken the law. All we have, all the bounties of His grace which we possess, we owe to God. The aggravating character of sin against such a God cannot be estimated any more than the heavens can be measured with a span. *God is a moral governor as well as a Father. He is the Lawgiver. He makes and executes His laws. Law that has no penalty is of no force.*

The plea may be made that a loving Father would not see His children suffering the punishment of God by fire while He had the power to relieve them. *But God would, for the good of His subjects and for their safety, punish the transgressor.* God does not work on the plan of man. He can do infinite justice that man has no right to do before his fellow man. Noah would have displeased God to have drowned one of the scoffers and mockers that harassed him, but God drowned the vast world. Lot would have had no right to inflict punishment on his sons-in-law, but God would do it in strict justice.

Who will say God will not do what He says He will do? (LDE 240, 241; emphasis added).

The paragraphs above say it all. And just to clarify, I am certainly not saying that we are the ones who should implement God's justice. In this life, that's what our police and courts are for. At the close of the millennium, God will do it—not human beings or even holy angels, and certainly not devils. And when the Lord does it, the recipients of His justice, and not the Lord, will bear the ultimate responsibility for their fate. It was their own choice that placed them outside the Holy City. The Man of Calvary did everything possible to save them from sin, but they refused His love and grace. They didn't have to be lost. Among the olive trees, and at the Place of the Skull, King Jesus drained that cup for them to the last drop. But they resisted His relentless love. Now it's forever too late.

"Then Death and Hades were cast into the lake of fire. This is the second death. And anyone not found written in the Book of Life was cast into the lake of fire" (Revelation 20:14, 15). "In the cleansing flames the wicked are at last destroyed, root and branch—Satan the root, his followers the branches. *The full penalty of the law has been visited; the demands of justice have been met; and heaven and earth, beholding, declare the righteousness of Jehovah*" (GC 673; emphasis added).

Eternal torment a heresy

Those "cleansing flames" completely annihilate the wicked. My little booklet *The Hot Topic of Hell* proves from the Bible alone that the lost won't sizzle forever, for how just would that be? Such a doctrine makes God look like a monster. Instead, when we examine all of the biblical evidence, we discover that the unsaved will become " 'ashes' " (Malachi 4:3); they will " 'perish' " (John 3:16); "into smoke they shall vanish" (Psalm 37:20); and they "shall be no more" (Psalm 37:10). The little lady told the truth when she wrote,

> It is beyond the power of the human mind to estimate the evil which has been wrought by the heresy of eternal torment. The religion of the Bible, full of love and goodness, and abounding in compassion, is darkened by superstition and clothed with terror. When we consider in what false colors Satan has painted the character of God, can we wonder that our merciful Creator is feared, dreaded, and even hated? The appalling views of God

which have spread over the world from the teachings of the pulpit have made thousands, yes, millions, of skeptics and infidels.

The theory of eternal torment is one of the false doctrines that constitute the wine of the abominations of Babylon, of which she makes all nations drink. Revelation 14:8; 17:2 (GC 536).

Thank God, "the heresy of eternal torment" isn't true. At the end of the millennium, this doctrine will perish too, along with the one who originated it. And when the smoke finally clears and Satan himself has disappeared for good, absolutely no Luciferian doubts about God's goodness will remain. No seeds of discontent will survive. Then the entire universe will breathe one collective, long-awaited and much-anticipated sigh of relief. It's over! Evil is finished, gone, eliminated, and permanently eradicated! Then "heaven and earth, beholding, declare the righteousness of Jehovah" (GC 673).

"The lake of fire" (Revelation 20:15) will complete its assignment. "The fire that consumes the wicked purifies the earth" (GC 674). Immediately following "the lake of fire" scene, the writer of the book of Revelation ecstatically reports,

> I saw a new heaven and a new earth, for the first heaven and the first earth had passed away. Also there was no more sea. Then I, John, saw the holy city, New Jerusalem, coming down out of heaven from God, prepared as a bride adorned for her husband. And I heard a loud voice from heaven saying, "Behold, the tabernacle of God is with men, and He will dwell with them, and they shall be His people. God Himself will be with them and be their God. And God will wipe away every tear from their eyes; there shall be no more death, nor sorrow, nor crying. There shall be no more pain, for the former things have passed away" (Revelation 21:1–4).

Praise God! No more heart disease, diabetes, arthritis, sore backs, or amputated limbs. No more divorce, child abuse, terrorist plots, funeral services, or cemeteries. No more heartbroken parents or kids clutching their tummies at night for want of food. No more lake of fire. And no more devil! "The former things have passed away."

When that time finally arrives, the Prince of peace will not only have paid the full price for our sins and satisfied justice, but He will have also erased evil entirely. Then He will re-create our world, making it into the pristine paradise it was before Lucifer seduced Eve through the snake. "The great controversy is ended. Sin and sinners are no more. The entire universe is clean. One pulse of harmony and gladness beats through the vast creation. From Him who created all, flow life and light and gladness, throughout the realms of illimitable space. From the minutest atom to the greatest world, all things, animate and inanimate, in their unshadowed beauty and perfect joy, declare that God is love" (GC 678).

When this time finally comes, there will be no more war about what God is like. The great war will be over, and those who remain will know beyond any shadow of doubt that "the LORD is good" (Psalm 100:5). As the redeemed forever contemplate the unfathomable mystery of their Savior's mercy, of the sword that fell upon Him in Gethsemane and at the Place of the Skull because of their sins, and of the fearful separation that the Father and the Son both endured to bind them to Their heart—in short, of Their character of love—they will continually discover that their Lord is even better than they thought.

Much better!

Let's be there!

---

1. James Strong, *The New Strong's Dictionary of Hebrew and Greek Words* (Nashville: Thomas Nelson, 1996), s.v. "opsonion"; emphasis in original.

2. *Merriam-Webster's Online Dictionary*, s.v. "arbitrary," http://www .merriam-webster.com/dictionary/arbitrary (accessed June 12, 2008).

For Further Thought and Discussion

1. What does the fact that there will be a day of judgment reveal about God's character?
2. What will the lost discover at the end of the millennium?
3. What revelation do you think will be most painful to them?
4. What do you think the saved will be thinking and feeling at the end of the millennium?
5. How will God Himself be vindicated at the end of the millennium?
6. After the great white throne judgment, Satan, his angels, and the lost will be destroyed, suffering the second death. Why has God waited so long to blot out evil?
7. Throughout eternity, sin will never again arise. Why not?
8. What do you think are some of the main reasons people choose not to give their lives fully to Jesus Christ?
9. Why is such holding back both dangerous and foolish?
10. If you are among the saved, what will you appreciate the most about your Savior as the years of eternity roll on?
11. Have you given your heart fully to Jesus Christ and trusted Him as your personal Savior? If not, why not?
12. What impressed you the most in this chapter, and why?

LIST OF ABBREVIATIONS FOR ELLEN G. WHITE REFERENCES

Books

1888   *The Ellen G. White 1888 Materials.* 4 volumes. Washington, D.C.: Ellen G. White Estate, 1987. (These books are paged as one volume.)

AA   *The Acts of the Apostles.* Mountain View, Calif.: Pacific Press® Publishing Association, 1911.

AG   *God's Amazing Grace.* Washington, D.C.: Review and Herald® Publishing Association, 1973; Hagerstown, Md.: Review and Herald®, 2001.

CH   *Counsels on Health.* Mountain View, Calif.: Pacific Press®, 1951.

COL   *Christ's Object Lessons.* Mountain View, Calif.: Pacific Press®, 1941.

CT   *Counsels to Parents, Teachers, and Students.* Mountain View, Calif.: Pacific Press®, 1943.

DA   *The Desire of Ages.* Mountain View, Calif.: Pacific Press®, 1940.

FCE   *Fundamentals of Christian Education.* Nashville: Southern Publishing Association, 1923.

FW   *Faith and Works: Sermons and Articles by Ellen G. White.* Washington, D.C.: Review and Herald®, 1979.

GC   *The Great Controversy Between Christ and Satan.* Mountain View, Calif.: Pacific Press®, 1950.

GW   *Gospel Workers.* Washington, D.C.: Review and Herald®, 1948.

HP   *In Heavenly Places.* Hagerstown, Md.: Review and Herald®, 1995.

LDE   *Last Day Events.* Boise, Idaho: Pacific Press®, 1992.

LHU   *Lift Him Up.* Hagerstown, Md.: Review and Herald®, 1988.

MB   *Thoughts From the Mount of Blessing.* Mountain View, Calif.: Pacific Press®, 1956.

PP   *Patriarchs and Prophets.* Mountain View, Calif.: Pacific Press®, 1958.

RC   *Reflecting Christ.* Hagerstown, Md.: Review and Herald®, 1985.

SAT   *Sermons and Talks.* 2 volumes. Silver Spring, Md.: Ellen G. White Estate, 1990–1994.

SC   *Steps to Christ.* Nampa, Idaho: Pacific Press®, 1981.

SDABC   *Seventh-day Adventist Bible Commentary.* 7 volumes. Washington, D.C.: Review and Herald®, 1980.

SM   *Selected Messages.* 3 volumes. Washington, D.C.: Review and Herald®, 1958–1980.

SP   *Spirit of Prophecy.* 4 volumes. Washington, D.C.: Review and Herald®, 1969.

T   *Testimonies for the Church.* 9 volumes. Mountain View, Calif.: Pacific Press®, 1948.

TM   *Testimonies to Ministers and Gospel Workers.* Mountain View, Calif.: Pacific Press®, 1944.

UL   *The Upward Look.* Washington, D.C.: Review and Herald®, 1982.

Magazines

RH   *The Advent Review and Sabbath Herald.*

ST   *Signs of the Times.*

THM   *The Home Missionary.*

Recommended Reading

The following articles are now available from the Biblical Research Institute of the General Conference of Seventh-day Adventists and may be accessed online: Frank Hasel, "The Wrath of God," http://www.adventistbiblicalresearch.org/documents/Wrath%20of%20God.htm, and Frank B. Holbrook, "Does God Destroy?" http://www.adventistbiblicalresearch.org/documents/Does%20God%20Destroy.htm.

For a deeper understanding of God's infinite love and goodness, we highly recommend Ellen G. White's *The Desire of Ages,* available at an Adventist Book Center near you, online at http://www.AdventistBookCenter.com, or call toll-free 1-800-765-6955.

To understand the biblical truth about hell and eternal fire, see Steve Wohlberg's booklet *The Hot Topic of Hell,* available through http://www.whitehorsemedia.com.

If you've appreciated this book, you'll want to read these other books by **Steve Wohlberg**:

From Hollywood to Heaven

This book reveals the gripping true story of Steve Wohlberg. He started out as a happy innocent Jewish boy growing up in the Hollywood Hills of Southern California. But by his teenage years, the allure of Tinseltown had drawn Steve into a dark and dangerous would of alcohol, drugs, and wild living. During the summer of 1979, he worked in the film industry and his downward spiral nearly cost him his life. Then God intervened. ISBN 10: 0-8163-21450. Also available on CDs.

Demons in Disguise
The Dangers of Talking to the Dead

Eventually, death knocks at every door. It often comes suddenly, without warning, and without mercy. Survivors miss the familiar voice, the personal touch, and the intimate companionship of deceased loved ones. Amid grief and pain many wonder, *Is it possible too talk to the dead?* Millions are answering, Yes. Unquestionably! A supernatural world does exist. But "beyond the veil," spirits can lie and ghosts can deceive. Steve Wohlberg provides explanations of apocalyptic phenomenon and provides solid biblical answers to the questions of life, death, and afterlife. ISBN 10: 0-7684-2491-7.

End Time Delusions
The Rapture, the Antichrist, Israel, and the End of the World

Millions of Christians sense we are nearing Jesus Christ's return. Yet when it comes to what the majority *thinks* will happen during earth's last days, and what the Bible *actually says* will occur, the difference is seismic. *End Time Delusions* exposes massive errors now flooding through the media. Wohlberg counters by letting the Bible speak for itself about the past, present, and future. ISBN 10: 0-7184-2960-9.